# Physical Characteristics of the Silky Terrier

(from the American Kennel Club's breed standard)

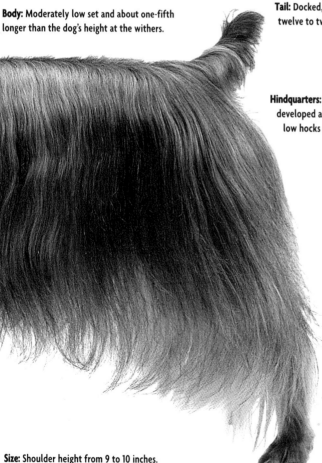

**Body:** Moderately low set and about one-fifth longer than the dog's height at the withers.

**Tail:** Docked, set high and carried at twelve to two o'clock position.

**Hindquarters:** Thighs well muscled and strong, but not so developed as to appear heavy. Well angulated stifles with low hocks which are parallel when viewed from behind.

**Color:** Blue and tan.

**Feet:** Small, catlike, round, compact. Pads are thick and springy while nails are strong and dark colored. The feet point straight ahead.

**Size:** Shoulder height from 9 to 10 inches.

# Silky Terrier

By Alice J. Kane

# Contents

KENNEL CLUB BOOKS: **SILKY TERRIER**
**ISBN: 1-59378-358-2**

Copyright © 2005 • Kennel Club Books, LLC
308 Main Street, Allenhurst, NJ 07711 USA
Cover Design Patented: US 6,435,559 B2 • Printed in South Korea

Photos by Isabelle Francais and Michael Trafford, with additional photographs by:
Norvia Behling, T. J. Calhoun, Carolina Biological Supply, Doskocil, James Hayden-Yoav, James R. Hayden, RBP, Carol Ann Johnson, Bill Jonas, Dwight R. Kuhn, Dr. Dennis Kunkel, Mikki Pet Products, Phototake, Jean Claude Revy, Dr. Andrew Spielman, Alice van Kempen and R. Willbie.

The publisher would like to thank all of the owners of the dogs featured in this book, including Tarianne Gallegos, Mrs. Marshall, Angelica C. Mazzarella, Rosemarie Napoleone, Jean Wagner and Doreen Weintraub.

Illustrations by Patricia Peters.

By any other name, the Silky Terrier is one of the world's most delightful little breeds, renowned for its soft, silky coat and its appealing temperament.

# SILKY TERRIER

The name game! Before we meet the Silky Terrier, let's take a moment to marvel at all of the names once assigned this breed. Today called the Silky Terrier in the United States and Canada, and the Australian Silky Terrier in Australia and the United Kingdom, the breed has also been called the following names: Australian Terrier, Soft or Silky Coated; Terrier, Soft and Silky; Sydney Silky Terrier; Victorian Silky Terrier; Soft as Silk; Broken-coated Toy Terrier and Broken-coated Blue Terrier. To further confound his fans, in Australia, the UK, the US and Canada, the Silky Terrier competes in the Toy Group, while in Europe and beyond, we find him in the Terrier Group. With over 100 years spent hammering out these "details," it is no wonder that such a delightful little dog was, for decades, a novelty to lovers of terrier types.

Ask breeders of the Silky Terrier to explain this merry mix of names and groups, and you will be told that this is a true "toy terrier"—the happy result of breeding terrier traits into an appealing, compact companion.

**THE SYDNEY RATTER**
Unlike other working Australian breeds, the Silky was one of the first Australian-created breeds developed for owners of apartments and cottages in Sydney. Excellent ratters, they soon became prized for their devotion to their family.

Known as the "Silky," the breed has a rich and somewhat mysterious history. Luckily, historians, determined to trace its origins, have uncovered compelling background on this dog. You, the new owner and happy book buyer, are the benefactor.

While origins may be debated, one fact stands without dissension: The breed is a "by-product" of the Australian

*The heavily coated and tiny Yorkshire Terrier is a prominent ancestor of the Silky Terrier.*

Terrier—a cross between terrier breeds established in Australia by settlers from England in the 19th century. Therefore, any discussion of the Silky Terrier, developed as a distinct breed in Australia after the turn of the 20th century, requires a study of the earlier Australian Terrier. Without records kept of those terrier breeds that created the Australian, historians have been forced to speculate. Some of the breeds involved include the Dandie Dinmont Terrier, Manchester Terrier, Skye Terrier, Norwich Terrier, Border Terrier, Cairn Terrier, Scottish Terrier, Fox Terrier and Airedale Terrier. Many regard a breed called the Rough or Broken-haired Terrier as the primary foundation stock.

Whatever the exact breeds, there is little doubt that the Australian Terrier resulted from stock produced by many types of terriers (particularly short-legged breeds) from Great Britain and the Continent. And with the semi-isolation of Australia from the British homeland, this distinctly "Australian-developed breed" became the available terrier blood to develop the Silky Terrier.

With the growing popularity of Australian Terriers, breeders introduced the Yorkshire Terrier in an attempt to improve color in the blue and tan dogs. The resultant litters contained some dogs that resembled the Australian Terrier, some that looked like the Yorkshire and some that retained qualities of both. But breeders were not out to produce "another Yorkshire." The goal was to breed a blue and tan silky-coated dog that was larger and less coated than the Yorkshire. This desired breed, the Silky Terrier, would derive his strength from his larger ancestor, the Australian Terrier, and his size and style from the smaller Yorkshire Terrier. Ideally, the breed would be suited to city and apartment dwellings, perfect pets and willing ratters for Australia's growing metropolitan cities.

The first standard for the Australian Silky Terrier was drawn up in Melbourne, Victoria, in 1904. A separate standard was created in Sydney, New South Wales, in 1906. The two states had two different standards for the one breed as well as slightly different preferences for type. The Victorians preferred the smaller Yorkie type of rich blue color; the New South Welshmen preferred honey-colored coats with light eyes.

In 1907, the newly developed breed, shown previously under the name of Terrier, Soft and Silky, was first exhibited at the Royal Dog Show in Sydney as the Sydney Silky Terrier. The following year, 1908, the Sydney Silky and Yorkshire Terrier Club

**ORIGINAL PURPOSE**
Although today's Silky is the ideal home companion, it is said that this inquisitive terrier was once considered a working dog, bred to control rodents.

was organized in the state of New South Wales, based on its first standard for the breed, adopted in 1906. That same year, 1908, in the state of Victoria, the Victoria Silky and Yorkshire Terrier Club was founded, issuing a different standard. Preferences for the silky coat type and color, eyes, size, etc., were established within each club, but a main purpose of both clubs was to draw up standards to distinguish between the Silky and Yorkshire for dog-show competition.

The ongoing crossbreeding between the Australian and Yorkshire and the subsequent backbreeding between the offspring produced a confusing array of dogs, often distinguishable only by weight. Under the clubs' new standards, a dog under 8 pounds would compete as a Yorkshire, one slightly larger competed as a Silky and the 12- to 14-pound dog appeared as an Australian Terrier. Allowing judges and breeders to develop specific conformation characteristics for these breeds, the clubs paved the way for the development of the distinctive appearance, as well as correct size of the breed, then known as the Sydney Silky. During that initial period,

### A DANDIE TOPKNOT

While the Silky is considered a blend of the Australian Terrier and the Yorkshire Terrier, the breed's distinctive topknot is said to have been acquired from the Dandie Dinmont.

breeders were permitted to register individual pups from litters as whichever breed they most resembled. It wasn't until 1932 that legislation was introduced to establish the three breeds and prohibit further crossbreeding.

Ironically, American interest in the Silky Terrier during the mid-1950s spurred interest in the breed in its native Australia. Most Silky Terriers were still found in Victoria and New South Wales, and it wasn't until 1956 that the breed dropped the "Sydney" in its name and became officially the Australian Silky Terrier. In March 1958, the Australian Silky Terrier Club of Victoria was formed, followed in December of 1959 by the Australian Silky Terrier Club of New South Wales. When the newly formed Australian National Kennel Council realized that the American Kennel Club was about to recognize the breed, the group worked speedily to compile its own standard. The result was a greatly improved standard that, within only a few years, vastly enhanced the Silky's soundness and size conformation.

It wasn't until the 1950s that the breed took the spotlight in Australia's Toy Group competitions. Aus. Ch. Bella Marie, offspring of Aus. Ch. Kansas Kiwi and Hillside Melody, and bred by the Norman Wenker family, was one of the first Silky Terriers to draw attention, winning high praise at the 1953 Royal Melbourne show. But one of the first Silkys to win Toy Groups and all-breed Best in Show honors was Aus. Ch. Milan Tony of Milan Kennels. He sired two dozen champions and his progeny are in today's winning lines in Australia. By the mid-60s, entries rose and the breed today remains a favorite in Australia's show ring—and in the home.

In Great Britain, the Silky Terrier arrived in the 1930s as a "new breed," still known as the Sydney Silky. A 1955 edition of *Hutchinson's Dog Encyclopaedia* pictures a Silky named Roimata Bon Ton, bred in New Zealand and a prizewinner at the Canterbury Kennel Club show in 1933. But it wasn't until the late 1970s that more Silkys were imported and the breed gained a following in Great Britain. Already smitten by the pint-sized Yorkshire Terrier, quite similar to the Silky in type, coat and color, British small-dog fanciers needed time and exposure to warm up to this "new" breed. But a good Silky, in type and temperament, is a dog to be reckoned with. Those fanciers with an eye to quality saw in the correct Silky specimens a formidable breed with great character and appeal.

Among the first British Silkys imported were two by Barbara Garbett: Apico Yatara Dutchboy and Glenpetite Lolita. Coolmine

**A SILKY ANCESTOR— THE AUSTRALIAN TERRIER**
Breed historians agree that the Silky emerged as a "by-product" during the establishment of the Australian Terrier. The earlier available history of the Australian Terrier is covered in *The Dog in Australasia*, by Walter Beilby, published in Australia in 1897.

Dockan, from Ireland, was imported by Linda Steward during this same period, as was Australia's Glenpetite Wataboy. The inaugural meeting of the Australian Silky Terrier Society was held in 1980, and today, there are many British Silkys of good quality, bred and shown by caring breeders committed to maintaining the correct type of the original imports.

**THE SILKY IN THE US**
Perhaps nowhere outside Australia are Silky Terrier fans as active as in the United States. Indeed, Australian fanciers admit

**THE RISE TO POPULARITY**
A 1954 cover photo of a Silky by well-known animal photographer, Walter Chandoha, captivated the American public. By 1959, they became the 113th breed eligible to receive American Kennel Club championship points and approximately 400–500 Silkys had been imported—a dramatic increase from the 30 or so in the US in 1954.

that it was the growing popularity and recognition of the breed in America that "shook up" their own breed clubs and spurred them to create a better working standard. The Australian standard was approved and adopted on March 30, 1959—and a copy was rushed to the American Kennel Club (AKC) in New York City, where, two weeks later on April 14, the AKC standard for the Silky Terrier was approved.

Many years before this, however, the first Silkys arrived in America. The breed's earliest pioneers, two Australian imports

in the early 1930s, Beaconsfield Smart Tone and Dream Girl, owned by Mrs. G. E. Thomas of Washington, DC, appeared on the February 1936 issue of the *National Geographic* magazine. The first Silky Terrier kennel was established in 1948 by Martha and Geoffrey Sutcliffe in Charlotte, North Carolina, whose story is legendary among American Silky fanciers. During World War II, Mr. Sutcliffe was taken prisoner in Shanghai. His wife flew to Australia to await his release, and during her stay, she fell in love with this intriguing national breed. Importing males, Kelso Dinkum and Wee Waa Aussie, along with a female, Glenbrae Sally, they established the Kanimbla kennel and bred a number of litters until the early 1970s. Their line comes down to present-day Silkys in the US.

In 1951, America's ongoing love affair with the Silky Terrier rocketed when respected Silky authority, Peggy Smith, then a newcomer to the breed, imported Brenhill Splinters, an Australian bitch. A male, Wexford Pogo, quickly followed in 1952, and over the next few years, Peggy Smith and her "Christmas pets" thrust this little little-known breed into the spotlight. Living in New York in 1954 and new to the sport of dogs, Mrs. Smith and her husband, Merle, made the decision to show. Their "pets" were of fine show stock and the Smiths entered Wexford Pogo at the Westchester Kennel Club show in the Miscellaneous Class. It was at this show that well-known animal photographer, Walter Chandoha happened upon Pogo's puppy, Redway Blue Boy. The photographer was so charmed that he had Mrs. Smith bring the pup to his studio. The resulting shot made the cover of *This Week* magazine and, within a month, Peggy Smith was receiving hundreds of inquiries from prospective Silky fans!

Over the next year, more than one hundred Silky Terriers were imported to the US. More and more photos appeared—silky-coated toys, perched beside their "rich and famous" owners—and dog people marveled at the country's captivation by the breed. (As for Wexford Pogo, one of the Silkys that started it all, he was

**POST-WAR EXPORTS**
Shortly after World War I, Australian Terrier and Silky Terrier puppies were sent around the globe. Hundreds of ships came into Australian harbors, where many Australian Silky Terrier puppies were purchased for 15 shillings each. The ships then returned to their homelands, where the puppies were sold.

declared by the late Fred David, Australia's Silky authority and judge, to be "the most representative Silky Terrier in the United States." Sire of numerous champions, he was "cover dog" for the first American book on the breed, published by Dr. Herbert Axelrod).

As the Silky grew prominent as pet and cover dog, those shown were entered in the AKC's Miscellaneous Class, essentially a showcase (and weigh station) for rare breeds. But it wasn't until

The diminutive Yorkshire Terrier and the rugged Australian Terrier gave rise to the Silky Terrier.

1955 that the Silky fired up the show world. Robert Garrett's Redway Splinter's Boy by Wexford Pogo out of Brenthill Splinters was the first of the breed ever entered at the Golden Gate show, the most prestigious West Coast dog show, held annually in San Francisco. The ensuing media blitz made this Silky the show's star attraction—the "rare dog breed"—and, just one year later, Golden Gate's Silky Terrier entry was up to 14. By year's end, large numbers competed in shows across the US, and by 1959, an estimated 400 to 500 dogs had been imported. From rare breed "cover dog" in 1954 to the 113th breed to earn acceptance by the AKC in 1959, the Silky Terrier had come a long way.

*The modern-day Silky Terrier enjoys moderate popularity around the world, from its native land "Down Under" to Europe, Asia and North America.*

Peggy Smith stayed active in the breed, compiling exhaustive records of imports, show history and pedigrees of American champions. Along with her own imports in the 1950s, Aus. Ch. Bowenvale Murray and Aus. Ch. Kelso Lady Susan dominated the show ring and influenced the look and future of the breed. As breed popularity increased, importing slowed down. American-bred Silkys appeared, perhaps none as prominent as Ch. Silkallure Casanova, owned and bred by Mona and Vic Bracco of California. Pronounced "unforgettable and irreplaceable," this well-beloved Silky accumulated over 100 Bests of Breed between 1964 and 1978. Even more impressive were his numerous Group placements and wins, rare then for the breed. He took Best of Breed at Westminster in 1966 and 1968 and captured a Group 4 in 1966. Add to all those achievements his record as top producer of champions, and he may well be called one of the most influential Silky Terriers in the breed's US history.

As for historian Peggy Smith, this devoted breeder can be most proud of her three Westminster Best of Breed Silky Terriers: Elsa Vinisko's Ch. Redway Lord Michael in 1962, her own Ch. Redway For Pete's Sake in 1975 and Ch. Redway Danny Boy O'Wexford in 1978—all owner-handled.

## SILKYS IN CANADA

Canada was a latecomer to the breed, but by the 1960s, fanciers fell under the Silky's spell and lost little time showing off their "new" breed. "Tinkerbelle," owned by Mrs. Marian Wait of New Brunswick and believed to have been bred by Mrs. W. Seagley of Topeka, Indiana, was the first known Silky in Canada. Mrs. Wait imported a few more, some from Australia, and with her total of seven Silkys by 1966, the breed became eligible to be added to the list of pure-bred dogs in Canada, having been passed by the Breed Recognition Committee of the Canadian Kennel Club (CKC). Asked by the CKC to submit a standard, Mrs. Wait presented an exact copy of the AKC standard for the Silky, which was accepted and adopted. The breed became known in Canada as the Silky Toy Terrier and, then, in 1988, the Silky Terrier.

One of Canada's top Silkys in the early years was Ch. Bonneen's Arunta Chieftain, known as "Amos." This personable dog, clever and of perfect type, was the first Silky to win Best in Show in both the US and Canada. Over his lifetime, he won over 100 Group firsts and a total of 33 Bests in Show. Each year, more and more Silkys are registered by the CKC. In 1987, devoted fancier, Dot Seabrook, established the first Silky club in Canada.

## THE BREED ON THE CONTINENT

Silky Terriers are shown in the Terrier Group at Fédération Cynologique Internationale (FCI) shows and in most European countries. But until 1961, Silkys were virtually unknown throughout Europe. Their introduction is attributed to an American, Robert Cooley of Coolaroo Kennels in California, who attended the 1961 Hofstad dog show in The Hague, Holland. Upon meeting Dutch fancier Anny Reijerink-Tibbe (now Anny Hartman-Tibbe of Germany), an exhibitor of Cairn Terriers, Cooley's enthusiasm for his Silkys prompted her to import two of his dogs, Coolaroo Karin and Coolaroo Pasja, both out of Australian champions. Captivated by the pair, Mrs. Reijerink-Tibbe exhibited the two Silkys all over Europe, winning new devotees to the breed everywhere they were shown.

In France, too, the first Silky Terriers came from Coolaroo Kennels, imported by Pierre Passerieux, Farmer's Kennels. As the breed grew in popularity, more

A toy terrier sound in mind and body is the goal of every Silky Terrier breeding program.

kennel of distinction at this time was Lillgardens, which imported a champion Silky from California's famous Coolaroo Kennels and three more bitches from Mona and Victor Bracco of California. All three dogs became international champions. Other famous winners at Nordic shows were Int. and Nord. Ch. Samiras Harrax, bred by Gunn-Britt Hjelm, and Int. Ch. Softhair's Silver Air, bred and owned by Britta Samuelsson. He was heavily line-bred to another top show dog, Aus., Swed. and Norw. Ch. Munbilla Rob Roy.

Through selective breeding and dedication to their dogs, Silky Terrier breeders throughout the world work to produce the same quality Silkys bred in turn-of-the-century Australia. Talk to a Silky breeder and you will be struck by a passion and commitment. Often, the dogs are owner-handled, their exhibitors as outgoing as the breed. With that same *joie de vivre*, they welcome newcomers willing to work together toward a toy terrier that continues to be sound in mind and body and possessed of a true Silky spirit.

were imported from Australia. One of France's earliest top winners was Int. Ch. Vetzyme de la Colline de Lorette, bred by Evelyne Pruvost and owned by Odile Tremblay.

Sweden's first Silky Terrier breeders were Anna Lisa and Elisabeth Westberg of Vaster-backens Kennels. Charmed by a Silky brought into Sweden, they imported Australian dog, Aus. Ch. Coolibah Cobbity, and bitch, Booroondara Steffe. With this pair, they whelped the first litter of their own breeding in 1965, and Cobbity quickly became a Swedish and Norwegian champion. Another

### A SILKY SUGARBABY
One of the Silky Terrier's most famous owners was Hollywood star Ann Miller. Asked on a visit to Australia what souvenir she would like to bring home, she replied, "I'd love one of those little Silky Terriers!"

Through the process of selective breeding, breeding the best bitches to the best dogs, using the standard as a guide, the Silky Terrier appears nearly the same from country to country.

# CHARACTERISTICS OF THE

# SILKY TERRIER

Brave, brawny fellow in the field? Or sweet, petite friend by the fire? In many homes, the sides are drawn when choosing the family dog. But what if both big- and little-dog characteristics could be found in one perfect package? The Silky Terrier is that pint-sized pup with great expectations. Spunky and self-possessed, with the sweet, generous nature of a companion dog, the Silky is a people-pleaser. "Look at me, Mom and Dad!" he implores. Racing, chasing, eager and alert—no

Silky's adventure is complete without you by his side.

Generations of breeding for gentleness of disposition have produced one of the most endearing yet spirited breeds in the purebred dog world. Many owners call their Silkys the "just right" dog—just the right size, just the right temperament, just the right companion. Sure of himself but eager to please, lively but not hyper, protective but not aggressive, the "big little" Silky ranks high as a household companion. And home is where he wants to be. His day does not begin until your arrival, his joy to see you surpassing all other events in his typical terrier day. Tail trembling, he lets you know, without a doubt, that you are number-one in his world!

With an eye to Australia's growth, early breeders sought a

Endearing and spirited, the Silky Terrier thrives as a companion dog, when surrounded by affection and kind treatment.

dog suited to city and apartment dwelling in the Sydney metropolis of New South Wales. His sturdiness and prowess for vermin-hunting derived from his larger terrier relation, the Australian Terrier. His small-dog appeal came from the diminutive Yorkshire Terrier. These remain qualities that fanciers look for in the breed: a small dog with the stamina of a large dog. He is not fragile; rather he is a lovable lapful. That he is a pretty dog is, no doubt, disarming, but even those who believe "it takes a big man to walk a little dog" would have no quarrel striding alongside a feisty Silky.

Not content with mere beauty and brains, breeders have produced an easy-maintenance dog. The Silky's non-shedding, odorless, single coat requires minimal grooming and trimming. A daily brushing and occasional snip will keep this blue and tan toy terrier looking handsome and well groomed.

The game Silky may still stalk a rat or snake, but this is a breed whose charm is in his devotion to his household. From years as a companion dog in the home, he craves civilization and socialization. Return his unwavering devotion and you will receive unconditional love.

The Silky does well with young and old, although, as with any small dog, children should be

**"WHO YOU CALLING 'TOY'?"**
The Silky Terrier has impressive physical strength for his size. Compared to other toy breeds, he is not fragile and his stamina makes him an energetic companion to children in the family.

quietly introduced and taught to show their canine companion kindness and respect. He will adore every member of his family unconditionally but may attach himself to a lucky favorite!

The Silky takes pride in his terrier heritage and a throaty "yip" will greet most would-be intruders at the door. Many a delivery person has backed behind the entryway, only to smile when this little vixen with the big voice presents himself. Most Silkys play polite hosts in the home, and even the more timid and reserved will respond to kind strangers once introduced.

His terrier background makes the Silky one of the sturdiest and hardiest of the Toy breeds, yet one

*The Silky Terrier is prized for his devoted nature, characterized by his territoriality and protectiveness (of his master, property and especially his own bed).*

of the smallest breeds in countries where he is placed in the Terrier Group. But size has never been a problem in his big-dog heart and he thinks nothing of playing in the "big-boy leagues." Feisty, demanding, fleet of mind and foot, the Silky plays boldly and assertively. He can be scrappy with brash dogs and his love of chasing will not enamor him to the family cat, rabbit or any other small mammal. Most do well in multiple-dog families, but they can be territorial and possessive of toys and food, and take little nonsense if challenged by other canines. Silkys can be acclimated to felines, though an owner should think twice about keeping

### A DISCERNING CHARACTER

With keen intelligence and inquiring eyes, the Silky is said to discern friend from foe. Observe and listen to your Silky. He has much to say, once you learn his language.

fancy rodents in the home of a Silky!

Take a front-row seat at playtime—the Silky's frenzied escapades around the yard are top-notch entertainment. But his high spirits should always be contained within a fenced area. His courage sometimes overrides his sense of safety, so owners should keep a sharp eye on his amusing shenanigans that can lead to trouble.

Owners agree that the breed's tremendous devotion is his most-prized quality. Talk to your Silky and he will understand far more than you realize. He is keenly alert, observing all, missing nothing. He is territorial and protective of you, and his purpose in life is to be your special friend. To deserve that trust, you will want to provide him with a life of emotional happiness and well-being. He should live in the home, actively involved in your activities. He is not a breed to be outside in a kennel, left to weather the boredom and "amuse himself." He enjoys the outside only with you by his side and he thrives on your undivided attention.

Along with his loving nature, the Silky has an innate intelligence. Describing his knack to discern friend from foe, owners claim that the Silky can detect attitude and vibes from people they meet—so don't be surprised to find your

Silky artfully assessing you! As is true for any intelligent breed, training and supervised play are crucial to getting the best out of your relationship. From the day that your puppy comes home, get him used to your touch and to being handled by all family members. Playtime is a great opportunity to communicate, stimulate his mind and seal the bond of your relationship. (Remember that exhausting a high-spirited puppy ensures you a better night's sleep!) We are all, human or canine, the product of our experiences. It is up to you to ensure that your companion enjoys a wealth of encounters that make him grow and thrive. Help your Silky reach his highest mental and emotional intelligence with simple socialization and loving discipline.

The smarter the dog, the greater his eagerness to "be the boss." While ceaselessly devoted, the Silky Terrier likes to get his own way; without training, he will orchestrate the household. Even a cute "petty dictator" can become a nuisance, warn devotees of the breed. Setting boundaries right at the beginning will give him reasonable guidelines and make him eager to please. Silky Terriers want to please, so half the battle is won. But he must learn that "No" means "no" and "Sit" means "sit." Give a command only once. Repeat it 100 times and

the savvy Silky will wait until you get to 99! Expect him to respond quickly, as long as he understands the command. If he doesn't, gently but firmly guide him. Always use positive reinforcement, never punishment. Silkys can be stubborn if "forced," so keep the training upbeat and fuel his natural curiosity. Don't think of training as a battle of wits. With the Silky, you've met your match, and only when you work as a team will your relationship blossom.

Training may also save your dog's life. Responding immediately to a command such as "Drop it" or "Down" has saved many dogs from poisoning or physical injuries on the street.

The Silky brings his eager-

## SILKY COLORATION
Silky pups are born jet black with tan markings. You may have to wait up until 18 months to know for certain the color of your adult dog.

**A TERRIER IN CLASS**
The "true terrier" may creep out when you work with your Silky in obedience. You cannot force a Silky to perform. He will shine when he wants to please you and when he believes he is having a good time. Try to find an obedience class that understands small dogs as well as terrier temperament.

ship of communication, trust and love is your reward for training.

A breed of stamina and vitality, the Silky keeps his puppy spirit throughout his life. When treated like a hardy dog, not a toy, he shows his true spirit and confidence. Don't let his diminutive size, lovely coat and engaging smile fool you. He is a high-energy dog and those who choose his companionship should consider their lifestyles and how much attention they can devote to his physical and emotional needs. Like the big dogs they emulate, Silkys are happiest when occupied and active. This is a terrier with the tenacity to romp with the big dogs, ward off intruders and find trouble if he thinks it looks like fun. An unsupervised, bored Silky may generate his own mischief, raiding papers and pantries and fulfilling his fiber needs with pieces of the backyard fence.

Exercise and stimulation are crucial to his well-being. A couple of daily walks, a sniff about the landscape and some rough-and-tumble family fun will make him a happy, most agreeable companion. Be aware that the Silky is a very curious fellow. Anytime your Silky is in an open area, he should at all times be kept on a lead. Unrestricted, who knows where his nose will take him!

There is plenty of fun to be had together. Dog clubs and

ness, vigor, alertness and concentration to his training. Your contribution to this team is persistence and patience. A polite, trained Silky is a companion in sync with you and your lifestyle. Spending time with you is his reward for learning, but a partner-

organizations offer a wealth of events where Silkys can show off. Obedience, agility and earthdog events are activities that stimulate his mind as well as his physical condition. Your Silky with do anything—with you by his side.

A vigorous breed, the Silky lives well into his teens and rarely needs medical treatment. For now, this toy terrier appears relatively free from the hereditary diseases that plague many other breeds. As with any dog, if you know your Silky well, you will be alert to any signals of ill health.

As your Silky Terrier ages, be alert for changes that could indicate health problems. Be especially attentive to checking for swellings under the skin.

**AFFECTION REQUIRED**

This is not a breed that tolerates long periods alone. Small in stature but high in energy, the Silky, left to himself, may generate some rather "creative" amusements! Provide him with a safe, dog-proof area when you are away. Better still, be generous of your time and affection.

Appetite, thirst, activity level, toilet habits, etc., are all signs of your dog's well-being. As he ages, watch for tooth, eye and ear problems, and swellings under the skin. Regular grooming sessions with your Silky will help you know his body so that you can quickly detect any changes that may need treatment. Fortunately, the Silky's health is as tenacious as his spirit, so expect your companion to enjoy a long and happy life with you.

Big-dog virtues in a diminutive companion: curiosity, courage, pride, protectiveness, dignity and confidence. Bred into the Silky Terrier through generations, these traits are as natural to the breed as his generous spirit. Many fanciers believe that once a Silky wins a place in your heart, there will always remain that place that only a Silky can fill.

# SILKY TERRIER

Each breed recognized by the American Kennel Club (or any other national kennel club) has an approved standard that tells us what the dog should look like and what we should expect from his temperament. A good breeder works to produce dogs that meet this standard, to ensure that the breed you admire today will continue to thrive and improve in future generations. While the "perfect" dog has yet to be born, those devoted to the Silky Terrier work tirelessly to produce it. They cherish the characteristics that make the breed different and are proud to tell you exactly what those are. The approved standard, meticulously put together by breed fanciers and historians, gives you a brief but all-important picture of the dog you are taking home.

The Silky standard defines a compact dog, firm in body with "sufficient substance to suggest the ability to hunt and kill domestic rodents," but it is "his inquisitive nature and joy of life" that make him an ideal companion. Petite only in size, the Silky is prized for his terrier characteristics—alertness, soundness and eagerness for action.

Dog shows are wonderful opportunities to observe ideal examples of the Silky Terrier. Not intended to be beauty competitions, dog shows determine how closely each dog in the ring conforms to the ideal as described in the breed standard. Here, you see the Silky as close to perfection as today's breeder can produce, not only in soundness and appearance but also in disposition and attitude. You see the qualities that distinguish the Silky from his relatives, the Yorkshire Terrier and the Australian Terrier, and every other member of the Toy Group, traits that show breeders and breeding at their best.

The Silky Terrier standard reflects the breeder's ideals and desire to perpetuate this happy, spirited little terrier through the generations. Equipped with an understanding of this standard and an overall picture of the breed, the new owner can know what to expect from his Silky and how to best meet his needs.

Here we present the American Kennel Club (AKC) standard for the Silky Terrier, as drawn up the Silky Terrier Club of America and approved by the AKC.

All dog shows revolve around the breed standard, the written description devised to steer breeders, judges and exhibitors towards the ideal or "perfect" breed represen- tative. Judges at dog shows appraise dogs by comparing them to the ideal dog as described in the standard.

A Silky Terrier of correct type, balance and structure.

## THE AMERICAN KENNEL CLUB STANDARD FOR THE SILKY TERRIER

**General Appearance:** The Silky Terrier is a true "toy terrier." He is moderately low set, slightly longer than tall, of refined bone structure, but of sufficient substance to suggest the ability to hunt and kill domestic rodents. His coat is silky in texture, parted from the stop to the tail and presents a well groomed but not sculptured appearance. His inquisitive nature and joy of life make him an ideal companion.

**Size, Proportion, Substance:**
**Size** Shoulder height from 9 to 10 inches. Deviation in either direction is undesirable. **Proportion** The body is about one-fifth longer than the dog's height at the withers. **Substance** Lightly built with strong but rather fine bone.

**Head:** The head is strong, wedge-shaped, and moderately long. **Expression** piercingly keen, **eyes** small, dark, almond shaped with dark rims. Light eyes are a serious fault. **Ears** are small, V-shaped, set high and carried erect without any tendency to flare obliquely off the skull. **Skull** flat, and not too wide between the ears. The skull is slightly longer than the muzzle. Stop shallow. The **nose** is black. **Teeth** strong and well aligned, scissors bite. An undershot or overshot bite is a serious fault.

**Neck, Topline and Body:** The **neck** fits gracefully into sloping shoulders. It is medium long, fine, and to some degree crested. The **topline** is level. A topline showing a roach or dip is a serious fault. **Chest** medium wide and deep enough to extend down to the elbows. The **body** is moderately low set and about one-fifth longer than the dog's height at the withers. The body is measured from the point of the shoulder (or forechest) to the rearmost projection of the upper thigh (or point of the buttocks). A body which is too short is a fault, as is a body which is too long. The **tail** is docked, set high and carried at twelve to two o'clock position.

**Forequarters:** Well laid back shoulders, together with proper angulation at the upper arm, set the forelegs nicely under the body. Forelegs are strong, straight and rather fine-boned. **Feet** small, catlike, round, compact. Pads are thick and springy while nails are strong and dark colored. White or flesh-colored nails are a fault. The feet point straight ahead, with no turning in or out. Dewclaws, if any, are removed.

**Hindquarters:** Thighs well muscled and strong, but not so

Silky Terrier head study of pleasing type and structure.

The hindquarters should show well muscled, strong thighs, and hocks parallel to each other.

developed as to appear heavy. Well angulated stifles with low hocks which are parallel when viewed from behind. **Feet** as in front.

**Coat:** Straight, single, glossy, silky in texture. On matured specimens the coat falls below and follows the body outline. It should not approach floor length.

On the top of the head, the hair is so profuse as to form a topknot, but long hair on the face and ears is objectionable. The hair is parted on the head and down over the back to the root of the tail. The tail is well coated but devoid of plume. Legs should have short hair from the pastern and hock joints to the feet. The feet should not be obscured by the leg furnishings.

**Color:** Blue and tan. The blue may be silver blue, pigeon blue or slate blue, the tan deep and rich. The blue extends from the base of the skull to the tip of the tail, down the forelegs to the elbows, and half way down the outside of the thighs. On the tail the blue should be very dark. Tan appears on muzzle and cheeks, around the base of the ears, on the legs and feet and around the vent. The topknot should be silver or fawn which is lighter than the tan points.

**Gait:** Should be free, light-footed, lively and straightforward. Hindquarters should have strong propelling power. Toeing in or out is to be faulted.

**Temperament:** The keenly alert air of the terrier is characteristic, with shyness or excessive nervousness to be faulted. The manner is quick, friendly, responsive.

## FAULTS IN PROFILE

Long back, low-set tail, rounded ears set too far apart, neck too short.

Roached back, straight shoulders, lacking rear angulation, narrow front.

Light eyes, straight shoulders, dip in topline behind shoulders, high in rear, too high on leg.

Ears too large and set too far apart, roached back, rear weak and lacking angulation, toes out in front.

# SILKY TERRIER

### SELECTING YOUR SILKY TERRIER

Assuming you have done research, gone to a couple of dog shows, met some breeders and studied the Silky Terrier standard, you should be ready to embark on the beginning of a 12- to 17-year relationship with a living, loving creature. You must also expect to embark on a relationship with the breeder. Choosing a Silky means committing yourself to the care and training of a lively, sensitive, people-loving breed. A good breeder will, and should, scrutinize you to see if you are up to the job. Just as you deserve a breeder with ethics and the best possible reputation, the breeder needs to know that his puppy will

*A dream task: selecting a Silky Terrier from a pair as gorgeous as this one. Invest time and energy in finding a well-bred, typical Silky Terrier puppy.*

**IN DUE TIME**
It will take at least two weeks for your puppy to become accustomed to his new surroundings. Give him lots of love, attention, handling, frequent opportunities to relieve himself, a diet he likes to eat and a place he can call his own.

have the family life he has been bred for. A loving relationship between owner and dog is all-important, but also of concern is how the dog will fit into your lifestyle. You will have to assure the breeder that you have the time and willingness to meet the needs of a dog that requires the love of his human family even more than he needs his own kind. Once the breeder "selects" you, you will be grateful for the relationship. This is the person you turn to over and over again to ask anxious questions, seek advice about small calamities and share joyous milestones.

The AKC and the Silky Terrier Club of America (STCA) can give you the names of reputable breeders in your region. STCA member

breeders are required to abide by a strict code of ethics. Dog shows are ideal places to observe well-bred Silky Terriers and to meet breeders who take great pride in their Silkys and enjoy sharing that enthusiasm with newcomers. Do visit with breeders after they are finished competing. Showing a dog takes preparation and concentration, and they will have more time to talk, answer your questions and show off their Silkys after the competition is over.

Once you know the Silky is for you, be prepared to wait for the breeder and dog you want. Good breeders often have waiting lists, but there is a reason for that. They have good dogs! The wait will be worth it. The wait may be longer depending on where you live. The breed has achieved moderate popularity in the US, so even if you cannot locate a breeder in your state, there should be some within a reasonable distance.

Choosing from a litter is an exciting, often emotional, time. While the breeder should help you select the puppy best for you, it is wise to know some of the physical traits to look for. A Silky puppy is born black and tan in color—tan on the lower legs and muzzle, and a spot of tan above each eye. The remainder of the body, head and foreface are black. As he matures, the black changes to silver, pigeon or slate blue,

**PUPPY APPEARANCE**
Your puppy should have a well-fed appearance but not a distended abdomen, which may indicate worms or incorrect feeding, or both. The body should be firm, with a solid feel. The skin of the abdomen should be pale pink and clean, without signs of scratching or rash. Check the legs to make certain that dewclaws were removed, if any were present at birth.

while the tan develops on the lower legs, ears, face and muzzle. The topknot will turn fawn or silver. This change in color may take up to two years.

The ears on a Silky's wedge-shaped head should be small and V-shaped, set high on the head and carried erect. The eyes, windows into the soul of the Silky, should be small and dark but piercingly alert in expression.

## YOUR SCHEDULE . . .

If you lead an erratic, unpredictable life, with daily or weekly changes in your work requirements, consider the problems of owning a puppy. The new puppy has to be fed regularly, social-ized (loved, petted, handled, intro-duced to other people) and, most importantly, allowed to go outdoors for house-training. As the dog gets older, he can be more tolerant of deviations in his feeding and relief schedule.

Eye rims should also be dark, either brown or black like the eyes. Teeth should be strong, straight up and down, meeting in an even, scissors bite, neither overshot nor undershot. The adult dog will stand 8–10 inches (20–25 cm) and weigh 8–10 pounds (about 4 kg). The Silky may be small, but he is not frag-ile and he has the stamina of a larger dog.

Temperament is, of course, what you and the breeder will be looking for in a companion dog. It makes good sense to tap the breeder's knowledge and intu-ition. The breeder has seen the litter interact and knows the bold puppy, scrambling for first dibs at human attention...or the timid puppy, sweet but needing a little persuasion to join in the fun. Some breeders find the males a bit more "affectionate," but all agree that both sexes are extremely loving. Male or female, the Silky is devoted and inquisi-tive, but each has his or her own unique character and approach to life. The breeder can help you select the pup that will blend best into your own personal lifestyle.

If the breeder has the puppies' parents on the premises, you should see them as well as the litter. Observing the sire and dam gives you an idea of what you can expect when your puppy grows into an adult dog. Since color takes up to two years to develop, seeing the parents could give you a preview of your mature Silky.

Breeders work diligently to produce well-bred, well-socialized litters, and their hope is to provide their puppies with the best possible new homes and lives. Many will shed a tear as they place their prize into your arms (you know you have a winner whenever this happens!). When you have been "chosen" to take home one of the puppies, you will have all of the breeder's blessings and support. Keeping up that relationship has rewards for both you and the breeder. Foster his Silky and you may well foster a lifelong friendship.

## COMMITMENT OF OWNERSHIP
After considering all of these factors, you have most likely already made some very important decisions about selecting your puppy. You have chosen the

Adopting a Silky Terrier is an exciting time, especially if you're going home with a "looker" like one of these darlings. Remember that the breed should be as sweet and affectionate as it is handsome.

Silky Terrier, which means that you have decided which characteristics you want in a dog and what type of dog will best fit into your family and lifestyle. If you have selected a breeder, you have gone a step further—you have done your research and found a responsible, conscientious person who breeds quality Silkys and who should be a reliable source of help as you and your puppy adjust to life together. If you have observed a litter in action, you have obtained a firsthand look at the dynamics of a puppy pack and, thus, you should have learned about each pup's individual personality—perhaps you have even found one that particularly appeals to you.

However, even if you have not yet found the Silky puppy of your dreams, observing pups will help you learn to recognize certain behavior and to determine what a pup's behavior indicates about his

### TEMPERAMENT COUNTS
Your selection of a good puppy can be determined by your needs. A show potential or a good pet? It is your choice. Every puppy, however, should be of good temperament. Although show-quality puppies are bred and raised with emphasis on physical conformation, responsible breeders strive for equally good temperament. Do not buy from a breeder who concentrates solely on physical beauty at the expense of personality.

temperament. You will be able to pick out which pups are outgoing, confident, shy, playful, friendly, dominant, etc. Equally as important, you will learn to recognize what a healthy pup should look and act like. All of these things will help you in your search, and when you find the Silky Terrier

**HANDLE WITH CARE**
You should be extremely careful about handling tiny puppies. Not that you might hurt them, but that the pups' mother may exhibit what is called "maternal aggression." It is a natural, instinctive reaction for the dam to protect her young against anything she interprets as predatory or possibly harmful to her pups.

The sweetest, most gentle of bitches, after whelping a litter, often reacts this way, even to her owner.

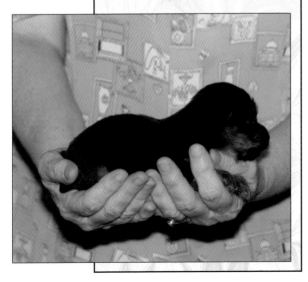

that was meant for you, you will know it!

Researching your breed, selecting a responsible breeder and observing as many pups as possible are all important steps on the way to dog ownership. It may seem like a lot of effort...and you have not even taken the pup home yet! Remember, though, you cannot be too careful when it comes to deciding on the type of dog you want and finding out about your prospective pup's background. Buying a puppy is not—or *should* not be—just another whimsical purchase. This is one instance in which you actually do get to choose your own family! You may be thinking that buying a puppy should be fun—it should not be so serious and so much work. Keep in mind that your puppy is not a cuddly stuffed toy or decorative lawn ornament, but a creature that will become a real member of your family. You will come to realize that, while buying a puppy is a pleasurable and exciting endeavor, it is not something to be taken lightly. Relax...the fun will start when the pup comes home!

Always keep in mind that a puppy is nothing more than a baby in a puppy-dog disguise...a baby who is virtually helpless in a human world and who trusts his owner for fulfillment of his basic needs for survival. In addition to food, water and shelter, your pup needs care, protection, guidance and love. If you are not prepared to commit to this, then you are not prepared to own a dog.

"Wait a minute," you say. "How hard could this be? All of my neighbors own dogs and they seem to be doing just fine. Why should I have to worry about all of this?" Well, you should not worry about it; in fact, you will probably find that once your Silky pup gets used to his new home, he will fall into his place in the family quite naturally. But it never hurts to emphasize the commitment of dog ownership. With some time and patience, it is really not too difficult to raise a curious and exuberant Silky pup to be a well-adjusted and well-mannered adult dog—a dog that could be your most loyal friend.

## PREPARING PUPPY'S PLACE IN YOUR HOME

Researching your breed and finding a breeder are only two aspects of the homework you will have to do before taking your Silky puppy home. You will also have to prepare your home and family for the new addition. Much as you would prepare a nursery for a newborn baby, you will need to designate a place in your home that will be the puppy's own. How you prepare your home will depend on how much freedom the dog will be allowed. Whatever

### ARE YOU PREPARED?

Unfortunately, when a puppy is bought by someone who does not take into consideration the time and attention that dog ownership requires, it is the puppy who suffers when he is either abandoned or placed in a shelter by a frustrated owner. So all of the "homework" you do in preparation for your pup's arrival will benefit you both. The more informed you are, the more you will know what to expect and the better equipped you will be to handle the ups and downs of raising a puppy. Hopefully, everyone in the household is willing to do his part in raising and caring for the pup. The anticipation of owning a dog often brings a lot of promises from excited family members: "I will walk him every day," "I will groom him," "I will house-train him," etc., but these things take time and effort, and promises can easily be forgotten once the novelty of the new pet has worn off.

## TIME TO GO HOME

Breeders rarely release puppies until they are eight to ten weeks of age. This is an acceptable age for most breeds of dog, excepting Toy breeds, which usually are not released until around 12 weeks, given their petite sizes. If a breeder has a puppy that is 12 weeks of age or older, he is likely well socialized and house-trained. Be sure that he is otherwise healthy before deciding to take him home.

you decide, you must ensure that he has a place that he can "call his own."

When you bring your new puppy into your home, you are bringing him into what will become his home as well. Obviously, you did not buy a puppy so that he could take control of your house, but in order for a puppy to grow into a stable, well-adjusted dog, he has to feel comfortable in his surroundings. Remember, he is leaving the warmth and security of his mother and littermates, as well as the familiarity of the only place he has ever known, so it is important to make his transition as easy as possible. By preparing a place in your home for the puppy, you are making him feel as welcome as possible in a strange new place. It should not take him long to get used to it, but the sudden shock of being transplanted is somewhat traumatic for a young pup. Imagine how a small child would feel in the same situation—that is how your puppy must be feeling. It is up to you to reassure him and to let him know, "Little bloke, you are going to like it here!"

## WHAT YOU SHOULD BUY

### CRATE

To someone unfamiliar with the use of crates in dog training, it may seem like punishment to

**PUPPY PERSONALITY**

When a litter becomes available to you, choosing a pup out of all those adorable faces will not be an easy task! Sound temperament is of utmost importance, but each pup has its own personality and some may be better suited to you than others. A feisty, independent pup will do well in a home with older children and adults, while quiet, shy puppies will thrive in homes with minimal noise and distractions. Your breeder knows the pups best and should be able to guide you in the right direction.

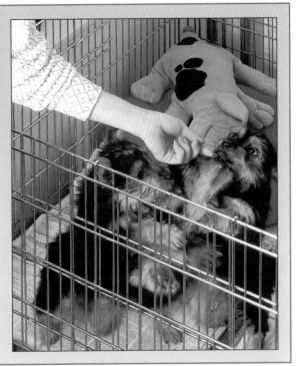

shut a dog in a crate, but this is not the case at all. More and more breeders and trainers around the world are recommending crates as preferred tools for pet puppies as well as show puppies. Crates are not cruel—crates have many humane and highly effective uses in dog care and training. For example, crate training is a very popular and very successful house-training method. A crate can keep your dog safe during travel and, perhaps most importantly, a crate provides your dog with a place of his own in your home. It serves as a "doggie bedroom" of sorts—your Silky can curl up in his crate when he wants to sleep or when he just needs a break. Many dogs sleep in their crates overnight. With soft bedding and his favorite toy, a crate becomes a cozy pseudo-den for your dog. Like his ancestors, he too will seek out the comfort and retreat of a den—you just happen to be providing him with something a little more luxurious than what his early ancestors enjoyed.

As far as purchasing a crate, the type that you buy is up to you. It will most likely be one of

PHOTO COURTESY OF DOSKOCIL.

small-sized crate is ideal for both the puppy and the adult Silky Terrier.

### BEDDING

A nice crate pad and a blanket in the dog's crate will help the dog feel more at home. This will take the place of the leaves, twigs, etc., that the pup would use in the wild to make a den; the pup can make his own "burrow" in the crate. Although your pup is far removed from his den-making ancestors, the denning instinct is still a part of his genetic makeup. Second, until you take your pup

the two most popular types: wire or fiberglass. There are advantages and disadvantages to each type. For example, a wire crate is more open, allowing the air to flow through and affording the dog a view of what is going on around him, while a fiberglass crate is sturdier. Both can double as travel crates, providing protection for the dog in the car. The size of the crate is another thing to consider. Puppies do not stay puppies forever, but the full-grown Silky is still a small dog. A

### CRATE-TRAINING TIPS

During crate training, you should partition off the section of the crate in which the pup stays. If he is given too big an area, this will hinder your training efforts. Crate training is based on the fact that a dog does not like to soil his sleeping quarters, so it is ineffective to keep a pup in an area that is so big that he can eliminate in one end and get far enough away from it to sleep. Also, you want to make the crate den-like for the pup. Blankets and a favorite toy will make the crate cozy for the small pup; as he grows, you may want to evict some of his "roommates" to make more room. It will take some coaxing at first, but be patient. Given some time to get used to it, your pup will adapt to his new home-within-a-home quite nicely.

home, he has been sleeping amid the warmth of his dam and litter-mates, and while a blanket is not the same as a warm, breathing body, it still provides heat and something with which to snuggle. You will want to wash your pup's bedding frequently in case he has an accident in his crate, and replace or remove any blanket or padding that becomes ragged and starts to fall apart.

## Toys

Toys are a must for dogs of all ages, especially for curious play-ful pups. Puppies are the chil-dren of the dog world, and what child does not love toys? Chew toys provide enjoyment for both dog and owner—your dog will enjoy playing with his favorite toys, while you will enjoy the fact that they distract him from your expensive shoes and leather sofa. Puppies love to chew; in fact, chewing is a phys-ical need for pups as they are teething, and everything looks appetizing! The full range of your possessions—from your favorite slipper to your new

Consider your Silky's full size when purchasing a crate. The crate and dog shown here are a good match, as the crate is of ample size to let the dog stand and stretch out fully.

## TOYS, TOYS, TOYS!

With a big variety of dog toys available, and so many that look like they would be a lot of fun for a dog, be careful in your selection. It is amazing what a set of puppy teeth can do to an innocent-looking toy, so, obviously, safety is a major consideration. Be sure to choose the most durable products that you can find. Hard nylon bones and toys are a safe bet, and many of them are offered in different scents and flavors that will be sure to capture your dog's attention. It is always fun to play a game of fetch with your dog, and there are balls and flying discs that are specially made to withstand dog teeth.

leather purse—are fair game in the eyes of a teething pup. Puppies are not all that discerning when it comes to finding something to literally "sink their teeth into"—everything tastes great!

As youngsters, Silkys are often aggressive chewers, but they eventually grow out of this. As adults, though, some Silkys can be dedicated chewers. Regardless, only the safest toys should be offered to your Silky at any stage of life.

Always take care when giving squeaky toys, for Silkys will usually remove squeaks and eyes immediately (reverting to their terrier instincts)! If a pup "disembowels" one of these, the small plastic squeaker inside can be dangerous if swallowed. Monitor the condition of all of your pup's toys carefully and get rid of any that have been chewed to the point of becoming potentially dangerous.

Breeders also advise owners to resist stuffed toys, because they can become de-stuffed in no time. The overly excited pup may ingest the stuffing, which is neither nutritious nor digestible.

Be careful of natural bones, which have a tendency to splinter into sharp, dangerous pieces. Also be careful of rawhide, which can turn into pieces that are easy to swallow and become a mushy mess on your carpet.

Purchase safe toys for your Silky Terrier. Soft, fuzzy toys are fine for puppies, provided that you supervise the game -playing. Adults may destroy soft toys as swiftly as they might a passing mouse.

Your Silky will need a light-weight yet sturdy leash for everyday walks and training.

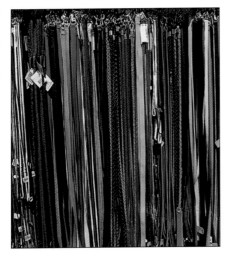

## LEASH

A nylon leash is probably the best option, as it is the most resistant to puppy teeth should your pup take a liking to chewing on his leash. Of course, this is a habit that should be nipped in the bud, but, if your pup likes to chew on his leash, he has a very slim chance of being able to chew through the strong nylon. Nylon leashes are also lightweight, which is good for a young Silky who is just getting used to the idea of walking on a leash. For everyday walking and safety purposes, the nylon leash is a good choice. As your pup grows up and gets used to walking on the leash, you may want to purchase a flexible leash. These leashes allow you to extend the length to give the dog a broader area to explore or to shorten the length to keep the dog near you.

## COLLAR

Your pup should get used to wearing a collar all the time since you will want to attach his ID tags to it. Plus, you have to attach the leash to something! A lightweight nylon collar is a good choice; make sure that it fits snugly enough so that the pup cannot wriggle out of it, but is loose enough so that it will not be uncomfortably tight around the pup's neck. You should be able to fit a finger between the pup and the collar. It may take some time for your pup to get used to wearing the collar, but soon he will not even notice that it is there. Choke collars are made for training but are not suitable for use on Toy dogs. Not only is the choke collar too harsh for small dogs, it also can damage the coat on longer-haired dogs.

## FINANCIAL RESPONSIBILITY

Grooming tools, collars, leashes, a crate, a dog bed and, of course, toys will be expenses to you when you first obtain your pup, and the cost will continue throughout your dog's lifetime. If your puppy damages or destroys your possessions (as most puppies surely will!) or something belonging to a neighbor, you can calculate additional expense. There is also flea and pest control, which every dog owner faces more than once. You must be able to handle the financial responsibility of owning a dog.

# CHOOSE AN APPROPRIATE COLLAR

The **BUCKLE COLLAR** is the standard collar used for everyday purposes. Be sure that you adjust the buckle on growing puppies. Check it every day. It can become too tight overnight! These collars can be made of leather or nylon. Attach your dog's identification tags to this collar.

The **CHOKE COLLAR** is designed for training. It is constructed of highly polished steel so that it slides easily through the stainless steel loop. The idea is that the dog controls the pressure around his neck and he will stop pulling if the collar becomes uncomfortable. This type of collar is unsuitable for use with the Silky.

The **HALTER** is for a trained dog that has to be restrained to prevent running away, chasing a cat and the like. Considered the most humane of all collars, it is frequently used on smaller dogs on which collars are not comfortable.

Select durable bowls that are chew-resistant and that can be cleaned easily. You may consider multiple water bowls so that you can keep one in each of the areas where your Silky spends time.

PHOTO COURTESY OF MIKKI PET PRODUCTS.

## FEEDING TIPS

You will probably start feeding your pup the same food that he has been getting from the breeder; the breeder should give you a few days' supply to start you off. Although you should not give your pup too many treats, you will want to have puppy treats on hand for coaxing, training, rewards, etc. Be careful, though, as a small pup's calorie requirements are relatively low and a few treats can add up to almost a full day's worth of calories without the required nutrition.

### FOOD AND WATER BOWLS

Your pup will need two bowls, one for food and one for water. You may want two sets of bowls, one for inside and one for outside, or at least an extra water bowl to put in the yard for your Silky. Stainless steel or sturdy plastic bowls are popular choices. Plastic bowls are more chewable. Dogs tend not to chew on the steel variety, which can be sterilized. It is important to buy sturdy bowls since anything is in danger of being chewed by puppy teeth and you do not want your dog to be constantly chewing apart his bowl (for his safety and for your wallet!).

### CLEANING SUPPLIES

Until a pup is house-trained, you will be doing a lot of cleaning. Puppy accidents will occur, which is acceptable in the beginning because the puppy does not know any better. All you can do is be prepared to clean up any accidents. Old rags, towels, newspapers and a safe disinfectant are good to have on hand.

### BEYOND THE BASICS
The items previously discussed are the bare necessities. You will find out what else you need as you go along—grooming supplies, flea/tick protection, baby gates to partition a room, etc. These things will vary depending on your situation, but it is important that you have everything you need to feed and make your Silky comfortable in his first few days at home.

## PUPPY-PROOFING YOUR HOME
Aside from making sure that your Silky will be comfortable in your home, you also have to make sure that your home is safe for your Silky. This means taking precautions that your pup will not get into anything he should not get into and that there is nothing within his reach that may harm him should he sniff it, chew it, inspect it, etc. This probably seems obvious since, while you are primarily concerned with your pup's safety, at the same time you do not want your belongings to be ruined. Breakables should be placed out of reach if your dog is to have full run of the house. If he is to be

limited to certain places within the house, keep any potentially dangerous items in the "off-limits" areas. An electrical cord can pose a danger should the puppy decide to taste it—and who is going to convince a pup that it would not make a great chew toy? Cords should be fastened tightly against the wall, out of the reach of the puppy. If your dog is going to spend time in a crate, make sure that there is

### INHERIT THE MIND
In order to know whether or not a puppy will fit into your lifestyle, you need to assess his personality. A good way to do this is to interact with his parents. Your pup inherits not only his appearance but also his personality and temperament from the sire and dam. If the parents are fearful or overly aggressive, these same traits may likely show up in your puppy.

Baby gates solve the problem of confining dogs to certain areas of the home. Once the puppy learns to accept the gates, he will never try to overcome them, even as a mature adult.

nothing near his crate that he can reach if he sticks his curious little nose or paws through the openings. Just as you would with a child, keep all household cleaners and chemicals where the pup cannot reach them.

It is also important to make sure that the outside of your home is safe. Of course your puppy should never be unsupervised, but a pup let loose in the

## TOXINS IN THE HOME

Scour your garage for potential puppy dangers. Remove weed killers, pesticides and antifreeze materials. Antifreeze is highly toxic and just a few drops can kill a puppy or an adult dog. The sweet taste attracts the animal, who will quickly consume it from the floor or pavement.

Chocolate contains the chemical thebromine, which is poisonous to dogs, although "chocolates" especially made for dogs are safe (as they don't actually contain chocolate) but not recommended. Any item that encourages your dog to enjoy the taste of cocoa should be discouraged. You should also exercise caution when using mulch in your garden. This frequently contains cocoa hulls, and dogs have been known to die from eating the mulch.

yard will want to run and explore, and he should be granted that freedom. Do not let a fence give you a false sense of security; you would be surprised how crafty (and persistent) a dog can be in working out how to dig under and squeeze his way through small holes, or to jump or climb over a fence. It doesn't take much of a hole for the tiny Silky to escape, and don't forget that earthdogs were born to dig. The remedy is to make the fence well embedded into the ground and high enough so that it really is impossible for your dog to get over it (about 4 feet should suffice). Be sure to secure any gaps in the fence. Check the fence periodically to ensure that it is in good shape and make repairs as needed; a very determined pup may return to the same spot to "work on it" until he is able to get through.

## FIRST TRIP TO THE VET

You have selected your puppy, and your home and family are ready. Now all you have to do is collect your Silky from the breeder and the fun begins, right?

### NATURAL TOXINS

Examine your grass and landscaping before bringing your puppy home. Many varieties of plants have leaves, stems or flowers that are toxic if ingested, and you can depend on a curious puppy to investigate them. Ask your vet for information on poisonous plants or research them at your library.

If you see your dog carrying a piece of vegetation in his mouth, approach him in a quiet, disinterested manner, avoid eye contact, pet him and gradually remove the plant from his mouth. Alternatively, offer him a treat and maybe he'll drop the plant on his own accord. Be sure no toxic plants are growing in your own yard or kept in your home.

Well...not so fast. Something else you need to prepare is your pup's first trip to the vet. Perhaps the breeder can recommend someone in the area who specializes in small terriers, or maybe you know some other Silky owners who can suggest a good vet. Either way, you should have an appointment arranged for your pup before you pick him up.

The pup's first visit will consist of an overall examination to make sure that he does not have any problems that are not

Many lovely, popular flowers can be harmful to dogs if ingested. Among the list of killer beauties is the poinsettia, a favorite holiday plant.

apparent to you. The vet will also set up a schedule for the pup's vaccinations; the breeder will inform you of which ones the pup has already received and the vet can continue from there. The

## HOW VACCINES WORK

If you've just bought a puppy, you surely know the importance of having your pup vaccinated, but do you understand how vaccines work? Vaccines contain the same bacteria or viruses that cause the disease you want to prevent, but they have been chemically modified so that they don't cause any harm. Instead, the vaccine causes your dog to produce antibodies that fight the harmful bacteria. Thus, if your dog is exposed to the disease in the future, the antibodies will destroy the viruses or bacteria.

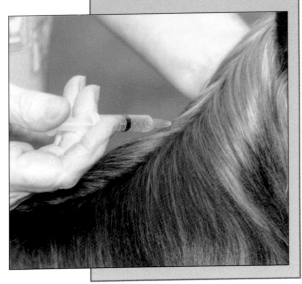

Silky can be sensitive to vaccinations and other injections; be sure to discuss this with your vet.

## INTRODUCTION TO THE FAMILY

Everyone in the house will be excited about the puppy's coming home and will want to pet him and play with him, but it is best to make the introductions low-key so as not to overwhelm the puppy. He is apprehensive already. It is the first time he has been separated from his dam and the breeder, and the ride to your home is likely to be the first time he has been in a car. The last thing you want to do is smother him, as this will only frighten him further. This is not to say that human contact is not extremely necessary at this stage, because this is the time when a connection between the pup and his human family is formed. Gentle petting and soothing words should help console him, as well as just putting him down and letting him explore on his own (under your watchful eye, of course).

The pup may approach the family members or may busy himself with exploring for a while. Gradually, each person should spend some time with the pup, one at a time, crouching down to get as close to the pup's level as possible while letting him sniff their hands and petting him gently. He definitely needs human attention and he needs to be touched—this is how to form an immediate bond. Just remember that the pup is experiencing a lot of things for the first time, at the same time. There are new people, new noises, new smells and new things to investigate, so be gentle, be affectionate and be as comforting as you can be.

## PUP'S FIRST NIGHT HOME

You have traveled home with your new charge safely in his crate or a friend or family member's lap. He's been to the vet for a thorough check-up; he's been weighed, his papers examined; perhaps he's even been vaccinated and wormed as well. He's met everyone in the family, including the excited children and the less-than-happy cat. He's explored his area, his new bed, the yard and anywhere else he's been permitted. He's eaten his first meal at home and relieved himself in the proper place. He's heard lots of new sounds, smelled new friends and seen more of the outside world than ever before.

That was just the first day! He's worn out and is ready for bed...or so you think!

It's puppy's first night and you are ready to say "Good night"— keep in mind that this is puppy's first night ever to be sleeping alone. His dam and littermates are no longer at paw's length and he's

### PEDIGREE VS. REGISTRATION CERTIFICATE

Too often new owners are confused between these two important documents. Your puppy's pedigree, essentially a family tree, is a written record of a dog's genealogy of three generations or more. The pedigree will show you the names as well as performance titles of all dogs in your pup's background. Your breeder must provide you with a registration application, with his part properly filled out. You must complete the application and send it to the AKC with the proper fee. Every puppy must come from a litter that has been AKC-registered by the breeder, born in the USA and from a sire and dam that are also registered with the AKC.

The seller must provide you with complete records to identify the puppy. The AKC requires that the seller provide the buyer with the following: breed; sex, color and markings; date of birth; litter number (when available); names and registration numbers of the parents; breeder's name; and date sold or delivered.

a bit scared, cold and lonely. Be reassuring to your new family member, but this is not the time to spoil him and give in to his inevitable whining.

Puppies whine. They whine to let others know where they are and hopefully to get company out of it. Place your pup in his new bed or crate in his room and close the crate door. Mercifully, he may fall asleep without a peep. When the inevitable occurs, ignore the whining; he is fine. Be strong and keep his interest in mind. Do not allow yourself to feel guilty and visit the pup. He will fall asleep eventually.

Many breeders recommend placing a piece of bedding from his former home in his new bed so that he recognizes the scent of his littermates. Others still advise placing a hot water bottle in his bed for warmth. This latter may be a good idea provided the pup doesn't attempt to suckle—he'll get good and wet and may not fall asleep so fast.

Puppy's first night can be somewhat stressful for the pup and his new family. Remember that you are setting the tone of nighttime at your house. Unless you want to play with your pup every night at 10 p.m., midnight and 2 a.m., don't initiate the habit. Your family will thank you, and soon so will your pup!

## PREVENTING PUPPY PROBLEMS

### SOCIALIZATION
Now that you have done all of the preparatory work and have helped your pup get accustomed to his new home and family, it is about time for you to have some fun! Socializing your Silky pup

gives you the opportunity to show off your new friend, and your pup gets to reap the benefits of being an adorable, intriguing creature that people will want to pet and, in general, think is absolutely precious!

Besides getting to know his new family, your puppy should be exposed to other people, animals and situations, but of course he must not come into

**MANNERS MATTER**
During the socialization process, a puppy should meet people, experience different environments and definitely be exposed to other canines. Through playing and interacting with other dogs, your puppy will learn lessons, ranging from controlling the pressure of his jaws by biting his littermates to the inner-workings of the canine pack that he will apply to his human relationships for the rest of his life. That is why removing a puppy from the litter too early can be detrimental to the pup's development.

close contact with dogs you don't know well until his course of injections is fully complete. Socialization will help him become well adjusted as he grows up and less prone to being timid or fearful of the new things he will encounter. Your pup's socialization began with the breeder, but now it is your responsibility to continue it. The socialization he receives in the first weeks after coming home is the most critical, as this is the time when he forms his impressions of the outside world. During the eight-to-ten-week-old period, also known as the fear period, the breeder takes extra care to make sure that the pup's interactions and experiences are gentle and reassuring. Lack of socialization can manifest itself in fear and aggression as the dog grows up. He needs lots of human contact, affection, handling and exposure to other animals.

### PROPER SOCIALIZATION
The socialization period for puppies is from age 8 to 16 weeks. This is the time when puppies need to leave their birth family and take up residence with their new owners, where they will meet many new people, other pets, etc. Failure to be adequately socialized can cause the dog to grow up fearing others and being shy and unfriendly due to a lack of self-confidence.

Once your pup has received his necessary vaccinations, feel free to take him out and about (on his lead, of course). Walk him around the neighborhood, take him on your daily errands, let people pet him, let him meet other dogs and pets, etc. Puppies do not have to try to make friends; there will be no shortage of people who will want to introduce themselves. Just make sure that you carefully supervise each meeting. If the neighborhood children want to say hello, for example, that is great—children and pups most often make great companions. However, sometimes an excited child can unintentionally handle a pup too roughly, or an overzealous pup can playfully nip a little too hard. You want to make socialization experiences positive ones. What a pup learns during this very formative stage will affect his attitude toward future encounters. You want your dog to be comfortable around

**PLAY'S THE THING**

Teaching your Silky to play with his toys in running and fetching games is an ideal way to help the dog develop muscle, learn motor skills and bond with you, his owner and master. He also needs to learn how to inhibit his bite reflex and never to use his teeth on people, forbidden objects and other animals in play. Whenever you play with your Silky, you make the rules. This becomes an important message to your dog in teaching him that you are the pack leader and control everything he does in life. Once your dog accepts you as his leader, your relationship with him will be cemented for life.

everyone. A pup that has a bad experience with a child may grow up to be a dog that is shy around or aggressive toward children.

CONSISTENCY IN TRAINING

Dogs, being pack animals, naturally need a leader, or else they try to establish dominance in their packs. When you welcome a dog into your family, the choice of who becomes the leader and who becomes the pack is entirely up to you! Your pup's intuitive quest for dominance, coupled with the fact that it is nearly impossible to look at an adorable Silky pup with his sparkling puppy-dog eyes and not cave in, give the pup an almost unfair advantage in getting the upper hand! A pup will definitely test the waters to see what he can and cannot do. Do not give in to those pleading eyes—stand your ground when it comes to disciplining the pup and make sure that all family members do the same. It will only confuse the pup when Mother tells him to get off the sofa when he is used to sitting up there with Father to watch the nightly news. Avoid discrepancies by having all members of the household decide on the rules before the pup even comes home...and be consistent in enforcing them! Early training shapes the dog's personality, so you cannot be unclear in what you expect.

COMMON PUPPY PROBLEMS

The best way to prevent puppy problems is to be proactive in stopping an undesirable behavior as soon as it starts. The old saying "You can't teach an old dog new tricks" does not necessarily hold true, but it *is* true that it is much easier to discourage bad behavior in a young developing pup than to wait until the pup's bad behavior becomes the adult dog's bad habit. There are some problems that are especially prevalent in puppies as they develop.

### NIPPING

As puppies start to teethe, they feel the need to sink their teeth into anything available...unfortunately that includes your fingers, arms, hair and toes. You may find this behavior cute for the first five seconds...until you feel just how sharp those puppy teeth are. This is something you want to discourage immediately and consistently with a firm "No!" (or whatever number of firm "Nos" it takes for him to understand that you mean business). Then replace your finger with an appropriate chew toy. While this behavior is merely annoying when the dog is young, it can become dangerous as your Silky's adult teeth grow in and his jaws develop if he thinks that it is okay to nip at and nibble on his human friends. Your Silky does not mean any harm with a friendly nip, but he also does not know how sharp his little terrier teeth really are.

### CRYING/WHINING

Your pup will often cry, whine, whimper, howl or make some type of commotion when he is left alone. This is basically his way of calling out for attention to make sure that you know he is there and that you have not forgotten about him. He feels insecure when he is left alone, when you

**PUP MEETS WORLD**
Thorough socialization includes not only meeting new people but also being introduced to new experiences such as riding in the car, having his coat brushed, hearing the television, walking in a crowd—the list is endless. The more your pup experiences, and the more positive the experiences are, the less of a shock and the less frightening it will be for your pup to encounter new things.

By the time your Silky is six months old, he should be completely accustomed to spending time in his crate. Make sure the crate is clean, cozy and kept away from any drafts.

## CHEWING TIPS

Chewing goes hand in hand with nipping in the sense that a teething puppy is always looking for a way to soothe his aching gums. In this case, instead of chewing on you, he may have taken a liking to your favorite shoe or something else that he should not be chewing. Again, realize that this is a normal canine behavior that does not need to be discouraged, only redirected. Your pup just needs to be taught what is acceptable to chew on and what is off-limits. Consistently tell him "No!" when you catch him chewing on something forbidden and give him a chew toy.

Conversely, praise him when you catch him chewing on something appropriate. In this way, you are discouraging the inappropriate behavior and reinforcing the desired behavior. The puppy's chewing should stop after his adult teeth have come in, but an adult dog continues to chew for various reasons—perhaps because he is bored, needs to relieve tension or just likes to chew. That is why it is important to redirect his chewing when he is still young.

are out of the house and he is in his crate or when you are in another part of the house and he cannot see you. The noise he is making is an expression of the anxiety he feels at being alone, so he needs to be taught that being alone is okay. You are not actually training the dog to stop making noise, you are training him to feel comfortable when he is alone and thus removing the need for him to make the noise. This is where the crate with cozy bedding and a toy comes in handy. You want to know that he is safe when you are not there to supervise, and you know that he will be safe in his crate rather than roaming freely about the house. In order for the pup to stay in his crate without making a fuss, he needs to be comfortable in his crate. On that note, it is extremely important that the crate is never used as a form of punishment, or the pup will develop a negative association with the crate.

Accustom the pup to the crate in short, gradually increasing time intervals in which you put him in the crate, maybe with a treat, and stay in the room with him. If he cries or makes a fuss, do not go to him, but stay in his sight. Gradually he will realize that staying in his crate is just fine without your help, and it will not be so traumatic for him when you are not around. You may want to leave the radio on softly when you leave the house; the sound of human voices may be comforting to him.

## DIETARY AND FEEDING CONSIDERATIONS

When you first bring your Silky puppy home, the breeder will encourage you to continue feeding the dog what he has been fed up to this point. Any changes to diet should be made gradually to avoid upsetting the puppy's digestion. Up to about four months old, your Silky will need about four meals a day. Feedings can then be reduced to three, and then two at around eight months. Adult Silkys normally thrive on one meal a day, with a few good, hard biscuits daily to keep the teeth clean.

With today's variety of nutritionally complete foods, choosing what you feed your Silky depends on what keeps your dog fit and what works best for you. Balance is key and meals should include proteins for growth and muscle, as well as carbohydrates, vitamins and minerals; the latter two are already found in many prepared dog foods. Dry food mixed with a canned or moist food satisfies most Silkys. While the breed is generally healthy with a good appetite, if you find yourself with a finicky eater, a little resourcefulness may be required. Patient trial and error to find your Silky's favorites or changing his feeding times will usually solve the dilemma. Table scraps—yes, it is tempting—are discouraged for this toy-sized terrier.

### STORING DOG FOOD

You must store your dry dog food carefully. Open packages of dog food quickly lose their vitamin value, usually within 90 days of being opened. Mold spores and vermin could also contaminate the food.

Some Silky breeders may encourage owners to supplement their dogs' diets with vitamins such as B for nerves and E for keeping the coat in good, healthy, shiny condition. But, overall, the Silky has no special feeding or dietary requirements, and feeding to ensure stamina and health is basically a matter of common sense and knowing your dog.

### TYPES OF FOOD

Today the choices of food for your Silky are many and varied. There are simply dozens of brands of food in all sorts of flavors and textures, ranging from puppy diets to those for seniors. There are even hypoallergenic and low-calorie diets available. Because your Silky's food has a bearing on coat, health and temperament, it is essential that the most suitable diet is selected for a Silky of his age. It is fair to say, however, that even experienced owners can be perplexed by the enormous range of foods available. Only understanding what is best for your dog will help you reach an informed decision.

Dog foods are produced in three basic types: dry, semi-moist and canned. Dry foods are useful for the cost-conscious, for overall they tend to be less expensive than semi-moist or canned. They also contain the least fat and the most preservatives. In general, canned foods are made up of

### FOOD PREFERENCE

Selecting the best dry dog food is difficult. There is no majority consensus among veterinary scientists as to the value of nutrient analysis (protein, fat, fiber, moisture, ash, cholesterol, minerals, etc.). All agree that feeding trials are what matter most, but you also have to consider the individual dog. The dog's weight, age and activity level, and what pleases his taste, all must be considered. It is probably best to take the advice of your veterinarian. Every dog has individual dietary requirements, and should be fed accordingly.

If your dog is fed a good dry food, he does not require supplements of meat or vegetables. Dogs do appreciate a little variety in their diets, so you may choose to stay with the same brand but vary the flavor. Alternatively, you may wish to add a little flavored stock to give a difference to the taste.

# A Worthy Investment

Veterinary studies have proven that a balanced high-quality diet pays off in your dog's coat quality, behavior and activity level. Invest in premium brands for the maximum payoff with your dog.

60–70% water, while semi-moist ones often contain so much sugar that they are perhaps the least preferred by owners, even though their dogs seem to like them.

When selecting your dog's diet, three stages of development must be considered: the puppy stage, the adult stage and the senior stage.

### PUPPY STAGE

Puppies instinctively want to suck milk from their mother's teats, and a normal puppy will exhibit this behavior from just a few moments following birth. If puppies do not attempt to suckle within the first half-hour or so, the breeder should encourage them to do so by placing them on the nipples, having selected ones with plenty of milk. This early milk supply is important in providing colostrum to protect the puppies during the first eight to ten weeks of their lives. Although a mother's milk is much better than any milk formula, despite there being some excellent ones available, if the puppies do not feed, the breeder will have to feed them himself. For those with less expe-rience, advice from a veterinarian is important so that not only the right quantity of milk but also that of correct quality is fed, at suitably frequent intervals, usually every two hours during the first few days of life.

Puppies should be allowed to nurse from their dam for about the first six weeks, although from the third or fourth week the breeder will begin to introduce small portions of suitable solid food. Most breeders like to introduce alternate milk and meat meals initially, building up to weaning time.

### GRAIN-BASED DIETS

Some less expensive dog foods are based on grains and other plant proteins. While these products may appear to be attractively priced, many breeders prefer a diet based on animal proteins and believe that they are more conducive to your dog's health. Many grain-based diets rely on soy protein, which may cause flatu-lence (passing gas).

There are many cases, however, when your dog might require a special diet. These special require-ments should only be recommended by your veterinarian.

Puppy and junior diets should be well balanced for the needs of your dog so that, except in certain circumstances, additional vitamins, minerals and proteins will not be required.

### ADULT DIETS

A dog is considered an adult when he has stopped growing. Although Silkys continue to develop physically until they are around three years of age, in general the diet of a Silky can be changed to an adult one at about 12 months of age. Again you should rely upon your vet or breeder to recommend an acceptable maintenance diet. Major dog-food manufacturers specialize in this type of food, and it is merely necessary for you to select the one best suited to your dog's needs. Active dogs may have different requirements than sedate dogs.

*Common sense tells you that a puppy requires a different diet than a full-grown adult, just as we feed human babies more delicate foods than adults consume.*

By the time the puppies are seven or a maximum of eight weeks old, they should be fully weaned and fed solely on a proprietary puppy food. Selection of the most suitable, good-quality diet at this time is essential, for a puppy's fastest growth rate is during the first year of life. Vets and breeders are able to offer advice in this regard. The frequency of meals will be reduced over time, and when a young Silky has reached the age of about 12 months, he can be fed an adult diet.

## "DOES THIS COLLAR MAKE ME LOOK FAT?"

While humans may obsess about how they look and how trim their bodies are, many people believe that extra weight on their dogs is a good thing. The truth is, pets should not be over- or under-weight, as both can lead to or signal sickness. In order to tell how fit your pet is, run your hands over his ribs. Are his ribs buried under a layer of fat or are they sticking out considerably? If your pet is within his normal weight range, you should be able to feel the ribs easily, but they should not protrude abnormally. If you stand above him, the outline of his body should resemble an hourglass. Some breeds do tend to be leaner while some are a bit stockier, but making sure your dog is the right weight for his breed will certainly contribute to his good health.

SENIOR DIETS

As dogs get older, their metabolism changes. The older dog usually exercises less, moves more slowly and sleeps more. This change in lifestyle and physiological performance requires a change in diet. Since these changes take place slowly, they might not be recognizable. What is easily recognizable is weight gain. By continuing to feed your dog an adult-maintenance diet when he is slowing down metabolically, your dog will gain weight. Obesity in an older dog compounds the health problems that already accompany old age.

As your dog gets older, few of his organs function up to par. The kidneys slow down and the intestines become less efficient. These age-related factors are best handled with a change in diet and a change in feeding schedule to give smaller portions that are more easily digested.

There is no single best diet for every older dog. While many dogs do well on light or senior diets, other dogs do better on special premium diets such as lamb and rice. Be sensitive to your senior Silky's diet and this will help control other problems that may arise with your old friend.

**WATER**

Just as your dog needs proper nutrition from his food, water is

**FEEDING TIPS**
- Dog food must be served at room temperature, neither too hot nor too cold. Fresh water, changed often and served in a clean bowl, is mandatory, especially when feeding dry food.
- Never feed your dog from the table while you are eating, and never feed your dog leftovers from your own meal. They usually contain too much fat and too much seasoning.
- Dogs must chew their food. Hard pellets are excellent; soups and stews are to be avoided.
- Don't add leftovers or any extras to commercial dog food. The normal food is usually balanced, and adding something extra destroys the balance.
- Except for age-related changes, dogs do not require dietary variations. They can be fed the same diet, day after day, without their becoming bored or ill.

an essential "nutrient" as well. Water keeps the dog's body properly hydrated and promotes normal function of the body's systems. During housebreaking, it is necessary to keep an eye on how much water and when your Silky is drinking, but, once he is reliably trained, he should have access to clean fresh water at all times, especially if you feed dry food. Make certain that the dog's water bowl is clean, and change the water often.

## EXERCISE

If your Silky should present you with a rat, remember, he is only doing his job! But, not to worry. First and foremost, he is a companion dog and may go through life never missing the chase. Still, he is an active fellow, not one to loll about on the couch for long, and you would be advised to keep him busy and in your company.

On path or pavement, your Silky has the pep for long, invigorating treks. If you are up for it, he is game. The heart of a hunter beats within his toy-sized chest and, given the opportunity for a country ramble, he may revert to his breeding and go to ground. Once his sensitive nose picks up the scent of vermin, he will put on quite a show, navigating bush and bramble, twists and turns.

The suburban Silky, with a fenced yard or run, should, simi-

## CHANGE IN DIET

As your dog's caretaker, you know the importance of keeping his diet consistent, but sometimes when you run out of food or if you're on vacation, you have to make a change quickly. Some dogs will experience digestive problems, but most will not. If you are planning on changing your dog's menu, do so gradually to ensure that your dog will not have any problems. Over a period of four to five days, slowly add some new food to your dog's old food, increasing the percentage of new food each day.

larly, be given opportunities for exercise. Being outdoors does not compensate for a couple of good walks a day on lead. A brisk trot through the neighborhood stimulates his terrier inquisitiveness and keeps him happier and fit.

Without a backyard, lucky urban Silkys are assured their daily walks! City streets and parks offer a banquet of scents and diversions, and your Silky will relish this time to explore and socialize. If your area has a dog run, where he is safe from escape or injury, do let him off the lead to enjoy a good scamper and scramble. Remember, though, to supervise his playtime. This mini-sprite may become protective when around strange dogs and, if he does, be assured that he has not read the "size" section of his breed standard.

Any exercise is fun for your Silky with you by his side. He will follow your lead, so keep him stimulated in body and spirit for the perfect partnership.

## GROOMING YOUR SILKY TERRIER

Compared with many other long-coated breeds and terriers that must be clipped, snipped and trimmed to perfection, the Silky Terrier requires a minimum of grooming and trimming. His single coat of fine, silky hair does not shed, and he is a naturally clean animal—bonuses for any

---

**DRINK, DRANK, DRUNK— MAKE IT A DOUBLE**

In both humans and dogs, as well as other living organisms, water forms the major part of nearly every body tissue. Naturally, we take water for granted, but without it, life as we know it would cease.

For dogs, water is needed to keep their bodies functioning biochemically. Additionally, water is needed to replace the water lost while panting. Unlike humans, who are able to sweat to dissipate heat, dogs must pant to cool down, thereby losing the vital water that their bodies need to regulate their body temperatures. Humans lose electrolyte-containing products and other body-fluid components through sweating; dogs do not lose anything except water.

Water is essential always, but especially so when the weather is hot or humid or when your dog is exercising or working vigorously.

---

owner. Unless you plan to show your Silky, you can probably do most of the grooming yourself. With his affinity for being by your side, it's easy to accustom him to being brushed and handled. He will look forward to your time together. It will also allow you to examine your Silky for any ear, eye or skin problems, a part of any good grooming routine.

A daily brushing promotes new hair growth and brings a

healthy shine to the coat. The tools you need are simple and easy to use—practice makes perfect. Use a natural bristle brush to clean and groom the coat and a metal comb to help take out tangles without tearing the coat. The mature coat is long, straight and silky. As your Silky's coat lengthens, the hair should be trained to part on the head and down the back to the root of the tail. A rat-tailed comb does the job nicely. Scissors and thinning shears are used to trim excess hair.

The Silky should be bathed "when dirty." Like many other terriers, they love a good roll in any "delightful smell" they can find outdoors. But when they "smell good to themselves," it's time for a bath! Use this tub time to take care of nails, teeth and ears. (Silky toenails are very quick to bleed, so keep a blood-clotting

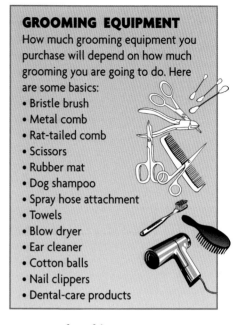

**GROOMING EQUIPMENT**
How much grooming equipment you purchase will depend on how much grooming you are going to do. Here are some basics:
- Bristle brush
- Metal comb
- Rat-tailed comb
- Scissors
- Rubber mat
- Dog shampoo
- Spray hose attachment
- Towels
- Blow dryer
- Ear cleaner
- Cotton balls
- Nail clippers
- Dental-care products

agent on hand.)

The Silky coat is of fine texture but there is plenty of it! He should have a clean ear, free of long hair. Excess, from the front and back of the ear, can be

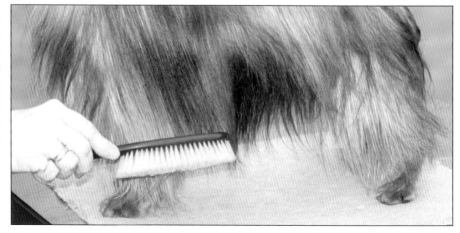

Brushing your Silky daily promotes new coat growth and a healthy shine to his soft coat. A distinct advantage to the Silky's coat is that it does not shed.

A natural bristle or another type of soft brush works well on the puppy's coat. Never brush too hard when grooming a young puppy. Make brushing a pleasant, non-stressful experience.

removed with small animal clippers, mustache trimmers, etc. Hair on the feet, likewise, should be trimmed with a pair of scissors to about "ankle" high. Also clean up the back side of the paws and between the pads.

The long hair of the body should come up to about the top of the foot. Unlike the Yorkie, the Silky's coat should not drag on the floor like that of a show Yorkie. If the tail hair needs trimming, snip to approximately 1 inch in length. The area between the eyes is the trickiest. Those long hairs should be trimmed so that the eyes are visible. From one inside eye to the other inside eye, make an inverted V between the eyes up to the part on the head. Any cleaning-up of excess hair can be done with thinning shears to provide a more natural look.

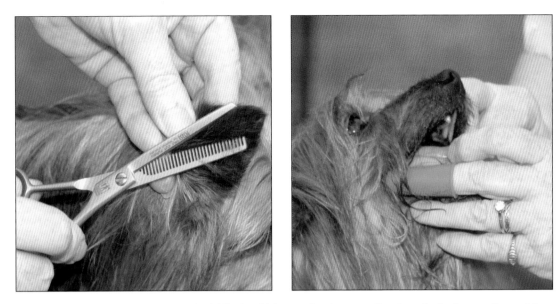

Grooming the Silky Terrier requires some specialized skills, though it is not as daunting or complicated as caring for the coats of many of the other terriers or toys. Top left: The ears can be tidied up. Top right: Tooth care is essential to healthy teeth and fresh breath This owner uses a tooth-cleaning tool that fits on her finger. Bottom left: Trimming the hair around the paws gives the Silky's feet a neat appearance. Bottom right: The tail benefits from a bit of tidying as well.

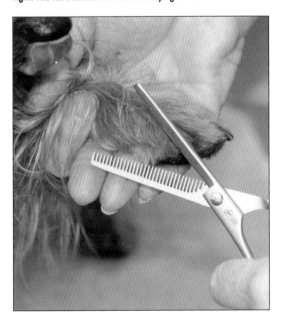

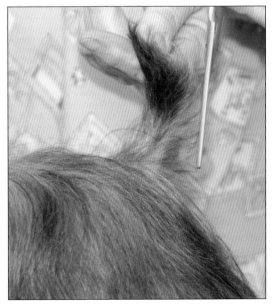

The Silky has a strong character. Tell him and show him what you expect from him at grooming time. If he seems a bit hesitant or feisty at first, try alternating a little massage along with the brushing or give him an occasional treat as you groom. Within a human family, keeping a youngster clean and healthy expresses the parent's love and concern for the child. The same is true for your canine family. He may try your patience, but the perceptive Silky appreciates the care you show him and recognizes grooming as an expression of your love. The day may soon come when

Use a wide-toothed comb gently on the puppy's coat, being careful not to pull or tug if you encounter a tangle.

Your local pet shop will have the grooming tools necessary for you to keep your Silky's coat in good condition.

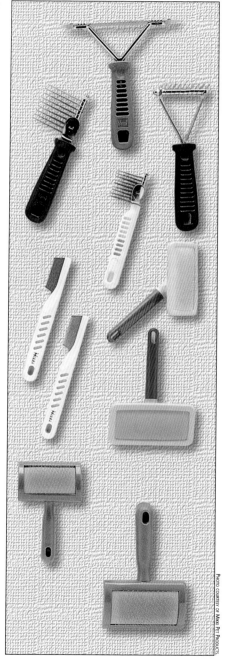

you get out his brush and he is already in position, eager and waiting for you!

**BATHING**

Dogs do not need to be bathed as often as humans, but bathing as needed promotes healthy skin and a clean, shiny coat. Again, like most anything, if you accustom your pup to being bathed as a puppy, it will be second nature by the time he grows up. You want your dog to be at ease in the bath or else it could end up a wet, soapy, messy ordeal for both of you!

Brush your Silky thoroughly before wetting his coat. This will get rid of most mats and tangles, which are harder to remove when the coat is wet. Make certain that your dog has a good non-slip surface to stand on. Begin by wetting the dog's coat. A shower or hose attachment is necessary for thoroughly wetting and rinsing the coat. Check the water temperature to make sure that it is neither too hot nor too cold.

Next, apply shampoo to the dog's coat and work it into a good lather. You should purchase a shampoo that is made for dogs. Do not use a product made for human hair. Wash the head last; you do not want shampoo to drip into the dog's eyes while you are washing the rest of his body. Work the shampoo all the way down to the skin. You can use this opportunity to check the skin for any bumps, bites or other abnormalities. Do not neglect any area of the body—get all of the hard-to-reach places.

Once the dog has been thoroughly shampooed, he requires an equally thorough rinsing. Shampoo left in the coat can be irritating to the skin. Protect his eyes from the shampoo by shielding them with your hand and directing the flow of water in the opposite direction. You should also avoid getting water in the ear canal. Be prepared for your dog to shake out his coat—you might want to stand back, but make sure you have a hold on the dog to keep him from running through the house and a towel nearby.

Be gentle and reassuring when clipping your Silky Terrier's nails. This is often not a Silky's favorite part of the grooming routine.

---

**PEDICURE TIP**

A dog that spends a lot of time outside on a hard surface, such as cement or pavement, will have his nails naturally worn down and may not need to have them trimmed as often, except maybe in the colder months when he is not outside as much. Regardless, it is best to get your dog accustomed to the nail-trimming procedure at an early age so that he is used to it. Some dogs are especially sensitive about having their feet touched, but if a dog has experienced it since puppyhood, it should not bother him.

---

**EAR CARE**
It is always necessary to keep a dog's ears clean, using a special cleaner, but take care never to delve into the ear canal, as this might cause injury to the dog. Fortunately, you can easily see into the Silky's ears for any sign of mites or infection.

**NAILS**
Never forget that toenails should be kept neat and that the Silky Terrier's toenails bleed very easily. Be especially careful when handling the Silky's feet. How

## Nail Clipping

Quick

Cut Line

Nail Casing

**DARK-COLORED NAIL**

With black or dark nails, like the Silky's, it's best to clip only a small bit of the nail at a time or to use a file where the quick is not visible.

**LIGHT-COLORED NAIL**

In light-colored nails, clipping is much simpler because you can see the vein (or quick) that grows inside the nail casing.

frequently the nails will need to be clipped will depend on how much your dog walks on hard surfaces, but they should be checked on a weekly basis. Canine nail clippers can easily be obtained from pet shops, and many owners find those of the guillotine design easier to use. A nail file can also be used to give a good finish to the nails. However, it is important to introduce a Silky to routine nail care from an early age, for many can be very awkward about this.

### TEETH
Teeth should always be kept as free from tartar as possible. There are now special canine tooth-cleaning agents available, including the basics, like small tooth-brushes and canine toothpaste.

### TRAVELING WITH YOUR DOG

#### CAR TRAVEL
You should accustom your Silky to riding in a car at an early age. You may or may not take him in the car often, but at the very least he will need to go to the vet and you do not want these trips to be traumatic for the dog or trouble-some for you. The safest way for a dog to ride in the car is in his crate. If he uses a crate in the house, you can use the same crate for travel.

Put the pup in the crate and see how he reacts. If he seems

uneasy, you can have a passenger hold him on his lap while you drive. Another option is a specially made safety harness for dogs, which straps the dog in much like a seat belt. Do not let the dog roam loose in the vehicle—this is very dangerous! If you should stop short, your dog can be thrown and injured. If the dog starts climbing on you and pestering you while you are driving, you will not be able to concentrate on the road. It is an unsafe situation for everyone—human and canine.

For long trips, be prepared to stop to let the dog relieve himself. Take with you whatever you need to clean up after him, including some paper towels and perhaps some old rags for use should he have a potty accident in the car or suffer from motion sickness.

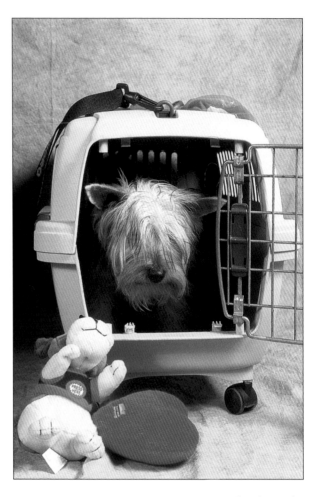

## LET THE SUN SHINE
Your dog needs daily sunshine for the same reason people do. Pets kept inside homes with curtains drawn against the sun suffer from "SAD" (Seasonal Affected Disorder) to the same degree as humans. We now know that sunlight must enter the iris and thus progress to the pineal gland to regulate the body's hormonal system. When we live and work in artificial light, both circadian rhythms and hormone balances are disturbed.

AIR TRAVEL
Contact your chosen airline before proceeding with travel plans that include your Silky. The dog will be required to travel in a fiberglass crate and you should always check in advance with the airline regarding specific requirements for the crate's size, type and labeling. To help put the dog at ease, give him one of his favorite toys

The safest way for any dog to travel by car is in his crate. This avoids unfortunate accidents and keeps the dog unharmed in case of a highway mishap.

## TRAVEL TIP

Never leave your dog alone in the car. In hot weather, your dog can die from the high temperature inside a closed vehicle; even a car parked in the shade can heat up very quickly. Leaving the window open is dangerous as well since the dog can hurt himself trying to get out.

in the crate. Do not feed the dog for several hours prior to checking in so that you minimize his need to relieve himself. Some airlines require you to provide documentation as to when the dog was last fed. In any case, a light meal is best. For long trips, you will have to attach food and water bowls to the dog's crate so that airline employees can tend to him between legs of the trip.

Make sure your dog is properly identified and that your contact information appears on his ID tags and on his crate. Many airlines permit small dogs to travel with their owners in the cabin, and the Silky is certainly a nice pocket-sized dog who can travel comfortably in his crate tucked under his master's seat. Discuss this option with your chosen airline and, if necessary, switch airlines until you find one that lets your Silky "fly the friendly skies" alongside you.

### VACATIONS AND BOARDING

So you want to take a family trip—and you want to include all members of the family. You would probably make arrangements for accommodations ahead of time anyway, but this is especially important when traveling with a dog. You do not want to make an overnight stop at the only place around for miles and find out that they do not allow dogs. Also, you do not want to reserve a place for your family without confirming that you are traveling with a dog because, if it is against the hotel's policy, you may end up without a place to stay.

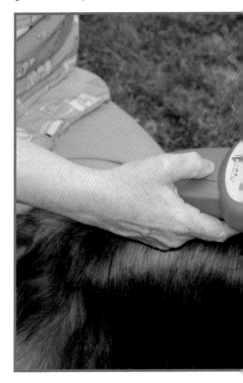

Alternatively, if you are traveling and choose not to bring your Silky, you will have to make arrangements for him while you are away. Some options are to take him to a friend's house to stay while you are gone, to have a trusted neighbor stop by often or stay at your house or to bring your dog to a reputable boarding kennel. If you choose to board him at a kennel, you should visit in advance to see the facilities provided, how clean they are and where the dogs are kept. Talk to some of the employees and see how they treat the dogs—do they spend time with the dogs, play

Your Silky should always wear a very light collar to which is attached his identification tags.

with them, exercise them, groom them, etc.? Also find out the kennel's policy on vaccinations and what they require. This is for all of the dogs' safety, since when dogs are kept together, there is a greater risk of diseases being passed from dog to dog.

## IDENTIFICATION
Your Silky is your valued companion and friend. That is why you always keep a close eye on him and you have made sure that he cannot escape from the yard or wriggle out of his collar and run away from you. However, accidents can happen and there may come a time when your dog unexpectedly gets separated from you. If this unfortunate event should occur, the first thing on your mind will be finding him. Proper identification, including an ID tag, and possibly a tattoo and/or a microchip will increase the chances of his being returned to you safely and quickly.

For the safety of your Silky Terrier, consider microchip implantation. Your vet can advise you about the most reliable systems and registries. The chip is read with a scanner that immediately identifies you as the owner.

Living with an untrained dog is a lot like owning a piano that you do not know how to play—it is a nice object to look at, but it does not do much more than that to bring you pleasure. Now try taking piano lessons, and suddenly the piano comes alive and brings forth magical sounds and rhythms that set your heart singing and your body swaying.

The same is true with your Silky Terrier. Any dog is a big responsibility and, if not trained sensibly, may develop unacceptable behavior that annoys you or could even cause family friction.

To train your Silky Terrier, you may like to enroll in an obedience class. Teach him good manners as you learn how and why he behaves the way he does. Find out how to communicate with your dog and how to recognize and understand his communications with you. Suddenly the dog takes on a new role in your life—he is clever, interesting, well-behaved and fun to be with. He demonstrates his bond of devotion to you daily. In other words, your Silky Terrier does wonders for your ego because he constantly

**REAP THE REWARDS**
If you start with a normal, healthy dog and give him time, patience and some carefully executed lessons, you will reap the rewards of that training for the life of the dog. And what a life it will be! The two of you will find immeasurable pleasure in the companionship you have built together with love, respect and understanding.

reminds you that you are not only his leader, you are his hero!

Those involved with teaching dog obedience and counseling owners about their dogs' behavior have discovered some interesting facts about dog ownership. For example, training dogs when they are puppies results in the highest rate of success in developing well-mannered and well-adjusted adult dogs. Training an older dog, from six months to six years of age, can produce almost equal results, providing that the owner accepts the dog's slower rate of learning capability and is willing to work patiently to help the dog succeed at developing to his fullest potential. Unfortunately, many owners of untrained adult dogs lack the patience factor, so they do not persist until their dogs are successful at learning particular behaviors.

Training a puppy aged 10 to 16 weeks (20 weeks at the most) is like working with a dry sponge in a pool of water. The pup soaks up whatever you show him and constantly looks for more things to do and learn. At this early age, his body is not yet producing hormones, and therein lies the reason for such a high rate of success. Without hormones, he is focused on his owners and not particularly interested in investigating other places, dogs, people, etc. You are his leader: his provider of food, water, shelter

**PARENTAL GUIDANCE**
Training a dog is a life experience. Many parents admit that much of what they know about raising children they learned from caring for their dogs. Dogs respond to love, fairness and guidance, just as children do. Become a good dog owner and you may become an even better parent.

and security. He latches onto you and wants to stay close. He will usually follow you from room to room, will not let you out of his sight when you are outdoors with him and will respond in like manner to the people and animals you encounter. If you greet a friend warmly, he will be happy to greet the person as well. If, however, you are hesitant, or anxious about the approach of a stranger, he will respond accordingly to you.

Once the puppy begins to produce hormones, his natural curiosity emerges and he begins to investigate the world around him. It is at this time when you may notice that the untrained dog begins to wander away from you and even ignore your commands to stay close. When this behavior becomes a problem, the owner

Bribery is no crime in the dog world! Use treats to train your young puppy and you will have a Silky who is always attentive and ready to obey.

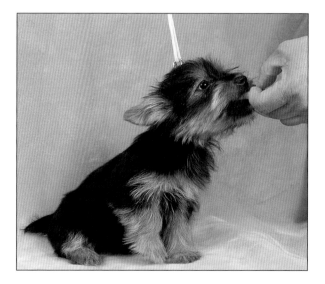

has two choices: get rid of the dog or train him. It is strongly urged that you choose the latter option.

There usually will be classes within a reasonable distance from you home, but you can also do a lot to train your dog yourself. Sometimes there are classes available but the tuition is too costly. Whatever the circumstances, the solution to training your Silky without formal lessons lies within the pages of this book.

This chapter is devoted to helping you train your Silky Terrier at home. If the recommended procedures are followed faithfully, you may expect positive results that will prove rewarding both to you and your dog. Your patience is of utmost importance, as your Silky's terrier background can sometimes lend a little stubbornness to the proceedings. Be consistent and praise often, and your Silky will be able to learn all of the commands necessary for basic obedience—and beyond!

Whether your new charge is a puppy or a mature adult, the methods of teaching and the techniques we use in training basic behaviors are the same. After all, no dog, whether puppy or adult, likes harsh or inhumane methods. All creatures, however, respond favorably to gentle motivational methods and sincere praise and encouragement. Now let us get started.

## HOUSE-TRAINING

You can train a puppy to relieve himself wherever you choose, but this must be somewhere suitable. You should bear in mind from the outset that when your puppy is old enough to go out in public places, any canine deposits must be removed at once. You will always have to carry with you a small plastic bag or "poop-scoop."

Outdoor training includes such surfaces as grass, soil and cement. Indoor training usually means training your dog to newspaper. When deciding on the surface and location that you will want your Silky Terrier to use, be sure it is going to be permanent. Training your dog to grass and then changing your mind two months later is extremely difficult for both dog and owner.

Next, choose the command you will use each and every time you want your puppy to void. "Hurry up" and "Potty" are examples of commands commonly used by dog owners. Get in the habit of giving the puppy your chosen relief command before you take him out. That way, when he becomes an adult, you will be able to determine if he wants to go out when you ask him. A confirmation will be signs of interest, such as wagging his tail, watching you intently, going to the door, etc.

## PAPER CAPER

Never line your pup's sleeping area with newspaper. Puppy litters are usually raised on newspaper and, once in your home, the puppy will immediately associate newspaper with voiding. Never put newspaper on any floor while house-training, as this will only confuse the puppy. If you are paper-training him, use paper in his designated relief area only. Finally, restrict water intake after evening meals. Offer a few licks at a time—never let a young puppy gulp water after meals.

# CANINE DEVELOPMENT SCHEDULE

It is important to understand how and at what age a puppy develops into adulthood. If you are a puppy owner, consult the following Canine Development Schedule to determine the stage of development your puppy is currently experiencing. This knowledge will help you as you work with the puppy in the weeks and months ahead.

| Period | Age | Characteristics |
|---|---|---|
| FIRST TO THIRD | BIRTH TO SEVEN WEEKS | Puppy needs food, sleep and warmth, and responds to simple and gentle touching. Needs mother for security and disciplining. Needs littermates for learning and interacting with other dogs. Pup learns to function within a pack and learns pack order of dominance. Begin socializing pup with adults and children for short periods. Pup begins to become aware of his environment. |
| FOURTH | EIGHT TO TWELVE WEEKS | Brain is fully developed. Needs socializing with outside world. Remove from mother and littermates. Needs to change from canine pack to human pack. Human dominance necessary. Fear period occurs between 8 and 12 weeks. Avoid fright and pain. |
| FIFTH | THIRTEEN TO SIXTEEN WEEKS | Training and formal obedience should begin. Less association with other dogs, more with people, places, situations. Period will pass easily if you remember this is pup's change-to-adolescence time. Be firm and fair. Flight instinct prominent. Permissiveness and over-disciplining can do permanent damage. Praise for good behavior. |
| JUVENILE | FOUR TO EIGHT MONTHS | Another fear period about 7 to 8 months of age. It passes quickly, but be cautious of fright and pain. Sexual maturity reached. Dominant traits established. Dog should understand sit, down, come and stay by now. |

NOTE: THESE ARE APPROXIMATE TIME FRAMES. ALLOW FOR INDIVIDUAL DIFFERENCES IN PUPPIES.

## PUPPY'S NEEDS

The puppy needs to relieve himself after play periods, after each meal, after he has been sleeping and at any time he indicates that he is looking for a place to urinate or defecate. The urinary and intestinal tract muscles of very young puppies are not fully developed. Therefore, like human babies, puppies need to relieve themselves frequently.

Take your puppy out often—every hour for a 12-week-old, for example, and always immediately after sleeping and eating. The older the puppy, the less often he will need to relieve himself. Finally, as a mature healthy adult, he will require only three to five relief trips per day.

## HOUSING

Since the types of housing and control you provide for your puppy have a direct relationship on the success of house-training, we consider the various aspects of both before we begin training. Taking a new puppy home and turning him loose in your house can be compared to turning a child loose in a sports arena and telling the child that the place is all his! The sheer enormity of the place would be too much for him to handle.

Instead, offer the puppy clearly defined areas where he can play, sleep, eat and live. A room of the house where the family

> ### CONSISTENCY PAYS OFF
> Dogs need consistency in their feeding schedule, exercise and relief visits, and in the verbal commands you use. If you use "Stay" on Monday and "Stay here, please" on Tuesday, you will confuse your dog. Don't demand perfect behavior during training sessions and then let him have the run of the house the rest of the day. Above all, lavish praise on your pet consistently every time he does something right. The more he feels he is pleasing you, the more willing he will be to learn.

gathers is the most obvious choice. Puppies are social animals and need to feel a part of the pack right from the start. Hearing your voice, watching you while you are doing things and smelling you nearby are all positive reinforcers that he is now a member of your pack. Usually a family room, the kitchen or a nearby adjoining

Purchase absorbent "potty-training" pads at your pet shop. These are a handy alternative to newspaper, especially useful for a small dog like the Silky or for city dogs.

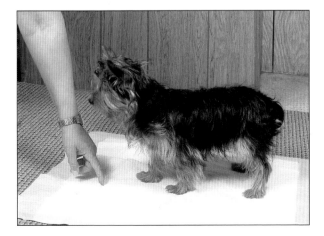

breakfast area is ideal for providing safety and security for both puppy and owner.

Within that room, there should be a smaller area that the puppy can call his own. An alcove, a wire or fiberglass dog crate or a gated corner from which he can view the activities of his new family will be fine. The size of the area or crate is the key factor here. The area must be large enough for the puppy to lie down and stretch out as well as stand up without rubbing his head on

*Select your Silky's relief surface based on what is available around your home. Once your pup learns to locate his spot, he will go there reliably time after time.*

the top, yet small enough so that he cannot relieve himself at one end and sleep at the other without coming into contact with his droppings.

Dogs are, by nature, clean animals and will not remain close to their relief areas unless forced to do so. In those cases, they then become dirty dogs and usually remain that way for life.

The designated area should contain clean bedding and a toy. Water must always be available, in a non-spill container, but be aware of when your Silky puppy is drinking so you'll know when he needs to "go."

### CONTROL

By *control*, we mean helping the puppy to create a lifestyle pattern that will be compatible to that of his human pack (you). Just as we guide little children to learn our way of life, we must show the puppy when it is time to play, eat, sleep, exercise and even entertain himself.

Dogs use their noses in many ways, one of which is to find a pleasing toilet area.

Your puppy should always sleep in his crate. He should also learn that, during times of household confusion and excessive human activity such as at breakfast when family members are preparing for the day, he can play by himself in relative safety and comfort in his designated area. Each time you leave the puppy alone, he should understand exactly where he is to stay.

Puppies are chewers. They cannot tell the difference between lamp cords, television wires, shoes, table legs, etc. Chewing into a television wire, for example, can be fatal to the puppy while a shorted wire can start a fire in the house. Crating the puppy keeps him safe when you're not there.

Furthermore, if the puppy chews on the arm of the chair when he is alone, you will probably discipline him angrily when you get home. Thus, he makes the association that your coming home means he is going to be punished. (He will not remember chewing the chair and is incapable of making the association of the discipline with his naughty deed.)

Other times of excitement, such as family parties, can be fun for the puppy, providing he can view the activities from the security of his designated area. He is not underfoot and he is not being fed all sorts of tidbits that will probably cause him stomach distress, yet he still feels a part of the fun.

**SCHEDULE**
A puppy should be taken to his relief area each time he is released from his designated area, after meals, after play sessions and

# THE SUCCESS METHOD

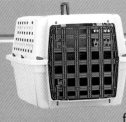

Success that comes by luck is usually short-lived. Success that comes by well-thought-out proven methods is often more easily achieved and permanent. This is the Success Method. It is designed to give you, the puppy owner, a simple yet proven way to help your puppy develop clean living habits and a feeling of security in his new environment.

## 6 Steps to Successful Crate Training

**1** Tell the puppy "Crate time!" and place him in the crate with a small treat (a piece of cheese or half of a biscuit). Let him stay in the crate for five minutes while you are in the same room. Then release him and praise lavishly. Never release him when he is fussing. Wait until he is quiet before you let him out.

**2** Repeat Step 1 several times a day.

**3** The next day, place the puppy in the crate as before. Let him stay there for ten minutes. Do this several times.

**4** Continue building time in five-minute increments until the puppy stays in his crate for 30 minutes with you in the room. Always take him to his relief area after prolonged periods in his crate.

**5** Now go back to Step 1 and let the puppy stay in his crate for five minutes, this time while you are out of the room.

**6** Once again, build crate time in five-minute increments with you out of the room. When the puppy will stay willingly in his crate (he may even fall asleep!) for 30 minutes with you out of the room, he will be ready to stay in it for several hours at a time.

## HOW MANY TIMES A DAY?

| AGE | RELIEF TRIPS |
|---|---|
| To 14 weeks | 10 |
| 14–22 weeks | 8 |
| 22–32 weeks | 6 |
| Adulthood | 4 |
| (dog stops growing) | |

These are estimates, of course, but they are a guide to the *minimum* number of opportunities a dog should have each day to relieve himself.

when he first awakens in the morning (at age 12 weeks, this can mean 5 a.m.!). The puppy will indicate that he's ready to "go" by circling or sniffing busily—do not misinterpret these signs. For a puppy around 12 weeks of age, a routine of taking him out every hour is necessary. As the puppy grows, he will be able to wait for longer periods of time.

Keep trips to his relief area short. Stay no more than five or six minutes and then return to the house. If he goes during that time, praise him lavishly and take him indoors immediately. If he does not, but he has an accident when you go back indoors, pick him up immediately, say "No! No!" and return to his relief area. Wait a few minutes, then return to the house again. Never hit a puppy or put his face in urine or excrement when he has had an accident!

Once indoors, put the puppy

in his crate until you have had time to clean up his accident. Then release him to the family area and watch him more closely than before. Chances are, his accident was a result of your not picking up his signal or waiting too long before offering him the opportunity to relieve himself. Never hold a grudge against the puppy for accidents.

Let the puppy learn that going outdoors means it is time to relieve himself, not play. Once trained, he will be able to play indoors and out and still differentiate between the times for play versus the times for relief.

Help him develop regular hours for naps, being alone, playing by himself and just resting, all in his crate. Encourage him to entertain himself while you are busy with your activities. Let him learn that having you near is comforting, but it is not your main purpose in life to provide him with undivided attention.

Each time you put a puppy in his own area, use the same command, whatever suits best.

Always clean up after your dog, whether you're in a public place or your own yard.

Soon he will run to his crate or special area when he hears you say those words.

Crate training provides safety for you, the puppy and the home. It also provides the puppy with a feeling of security, and that helps the puppy achieve self-confidence and clean habits. Remember that one of the primary ingredients in house-training your puppy is control. Regardless of your lifestyle, there will always be occasions when you will need to have a place where your dog can stay and be happy and safe. Crate training is the answer for now and in the future.

In conclusion, a few key

elements are really all you need for a successful house-training method—consistency, frequency, praise, control and supervision. By following these procedures with a normal, healthy puppy, you and the puppy will soon be past the stage of "accidents" and ready to move on to a clean and rewarding life together.

**ROLES OF DISCIPLINE, REWARD AND PUNISHMENT**
Discipline, training one to act in accordance with rules, brings order to life. It is as simple as that. Without discipline, particularly in a group society, chaos reigns supreme and the group will eventually perish. Humans and canines are social animals and need some form of discipline in order to function effectively. They must procure food, reproduce to keep the species going and protect their home base and their young.

If there were no discipline in the lives of social animals, they would eventually die from starvation and/or predation by other

The down position can only be mastered once the puppy learns to trust his master. Since it is a submissive posture in canine body language, the owner must approach this lesson gently with care.

stronger animals. In the case of domestic canines, dogs need discipline in their lives in order to understand how their pack (you and other family members) functions and how they must act in order to survive.

A large humane society in a highly populated area recently surveyed dog owners regarding their satisfaction with their relationships with their dogs. People who had trained their dogs were 75% more satisfied with their pets than those who had never trained their dogs.

Dr. Edward Thorndike, a renowned psychologist, established *Thorndike's Theory of Learning*, which states that a behavior that results in a pleasant event tends to be repeated. A behavior that results in an unpleasant event, likewise, tends not to be repeated. It is this theory on which training methods are based today. For example, if you manipulate a dog to perform a specific behavior and reward him for doing it, he is likely to do it again because he enjoyed the end result.

Occasionally, punishment, a penalty inflicted for an offense, is necessary. The best type of punishment often comes from an outside source. For example, a child is told not to touch the stove because he may get burned. He disobeys and touches the stove. In doing so, he receives a burn. From that time on, he respects the heat of the stove and avoids contact with it. Therefore, a behavior that results in an unpleasant event tends not to be repeated.

A good example of a dog learning the hard way is the dog who chases the house cat. He is told many times to leave the cat

## FEAR AGGRESSION

Pups who are subjected to physical abuse during training commonly end up with behavioral problems as adults. One common result of abuse is fear aggression, in which a dog will lash out, bare his teeth, snarl and finally bite someone by whom he feels threatened. For example, your daughter may be playing with the dog one afternoon. As they play hide-and-seek, she backs the dog into a corner and, as she attempts to tease him playfully, he bites her hand. Examine the cause of this behavior. Did your daughter ever hit the dog? Did someone who resembles your daughter hit or scream at the dog?

Fortunately, fear aggression is relatively easy to correct. Have your daughter engage in only positive activities with the dog, such as feeding, petting and walking. She should not give any corrections or negative feedback. If the dog still growls or cowers away from her, allow someone else to accompany them. After approximately one week, the dog should feel that he can rely on her for many positive things, and he will also be prevented from reacting fearfully towards anyone who might resemble her.

alone, yet he persists in teasing the cat. Then, one day he begins chasing the cat but the cat turns and swipes a claw across the dog's face, leaving him with a painful gash on his nose. The final result is that the dog stops chasing the cat.

## TRAINING EQUIPMENT

### COLLAR AND LEASH
For a Silky Terrier, the collar and lead that you use for training must be one with which you are easily able to work, not too heavy for the dog and perfectly safe.

### THE STUDENT'S STRESS TEST
During training sessions, you must be able to recognize signs of stress in your dog such as:
• tucking his tail between his legs
• lowering his head
• shivering or trembling
• standing completely still or running away
• panting and/or salivating
• avoiding eye contact
• flattening his ears back
• urinating submissively
• rolling over and lifting a leg
• grinning or baring teeth
• aggression when restrained
If your four-legged student displays these signs, he may just be nervous or intimidated. The training session may have been too lengthy, with not enough praise and affirmation. Stop for the day and try again tomorrow.

### TREATS
Have a bag of treats on hand. Something nutritious and easy to swallow works best. Use a soft treat, a chunk of cheese or a piece of cooked chicken rather than a dry biscuit. By the time the dog has finished chewing a dry treat, he will forget why he is being rewarded in the first place! Using food rewards will not teach a dog to beg at the table—the only way to teach a dog to beg at the table is to give him food from the table. In training, rewarding the dog with a food treat will help him associate praise and the treats with learning new behaviors that obviously please his owner.

## TRAINING BEGINS: ASK THE DOG A QUESTION
In order to teach your dog anything, you must first get his attention. After all, he cannot learn anything if he is looking away from you with his mind on something else.

To get his attention, ask him "School?" and immediately walk over to him and give him a treat as you tell him "Good dog." Wait a minute or two and repeat the routine, this time with a treat in your hand as you approach within a foot of the dog. Do not go directly to him, but stop about a foot short of him and hold out the treat as you ask "School?" He will see you approaching with a treat in your hand and most likely

Select a collar and lead for your Silky that fits properly and is strong enough to control the dog, while comfortable for the dog. Pet shops sell a variety of leads that may ignite your fancy—or patriotism!

Every dog should be trained to sit upon command. It is the easiest of all the mandatory exercises for your Silky to master.

probably be getting the idea that if he pays attention to you, especially when you ask that question, it will pay off in treats and enjoyable activities for him. In other words, he learns that "school" means doing great things with you that are fun and result in positive attention for him.

Remember that the dog does not understand your verbal language; he only recognizes sounds. Your question translates to a series of sounds for him, and those sounds become the signal to go to you and pay attention; if he does, he will get to interact with you plus receive treats and praise.

## THE BASIC COMMANDS

### TEACHING SIT
Now that you have the dog's attention, attach his lead and hold it in your left hand and a food treat in your right. Place your food hand at the dog's nose and let him lick the treat but not take it from you. Say "Sit" and slowly raise your food hand from in front of the dog's nose up over his head so that he is looking at the ceiling. As he bends his head upward, he will have to bend his knees to maintain his balance. As he bends his knees, he will assume a sit position. At that point, release the food treat and praise lavishly with comments such as "Good dog! Good sit!"

begin walking toward you. As you meet, give him the treat and praise again.

The third time, ask the question, have a treat in your hand and walk only a short distance toward the dog so that he must walk almost all the way to you. As he reaches you, give him the treat and praise again.

By this time, the dog will

Remember to always praise enthusiastically, because dogs relish verbal praise from their owners and feel so proud of themselves whenever they accomplish a behavior.

As a sidebar, you will not use food forever in getting the dog to obey your commands. Food is only used to teach new behaviors, and once the dog knows what you want when you give a specific command, you will wean him off the food treats but still maintain the verbal praise. After all, you will always have your voice with you, and there will be many times when you have no food rewards but expect the dog to obey.

### TEACHING DOWN

Teaching the down exercise is easy when you understand how the dog perceives the down position, and it is very difficult when you do not. Dogs perceive the down position as a submissive one; therefore, teaching the down exercise using a forceful method can sometimes make the dog develop such a fear of the down that he either runs away when you say "Down" or he attempts to snap at the person who tries to force him down.

Have the dog sit close alongside your left leg, facing in the same direction as you are. Hold the lead in your left hand and a food treat in your right. Now

**DOUBLE JEOPARDY**
A dog in jeopardy never lies down. He stays alert on his feet because instinct tells him that he may have to run away or fight for his survival. Therefore, if a dog feels threatened or anxious, he will not lie down. Consequently, it is important to keep the dog calm and relaxed as he learns the down exercise.

dog to lie down close to your left leg rather than to swing away from your side when he drops.

Now place the food hand at the dog's nose, say "Down" very softly (almost a whisper), and slowly lower the food hand to the dog's front feet. When the food hand reaches the floor, begin moving it forward along the floor in front of the dog. Keep talking softly to the dog, saying things like, "Do you want this treat? You can do this, good dog." Your reassuring tone of voice will help calm the dog as he tries to follow the food hand in order to get the treat.

When the dog's elbows touch the floor, release the food and praise softly. Try to get the dog to maintain that down position for several seconds before you let him sit up again. The goal here is to get the dog to settle down and not feel threatened in the down position.

### TEACHING STAY
It is easy to teach the dog to stay in either a sit or a down position. Again, we use food and praise during the teaching process as we help the dog to understand exactly what it is that we are expecting him to do.

To teach the sit/stay, start with the dog sitting on your left side as before and hold the lead in your left hand. Have a food treat in your right hand and place

### COMMAND STANCE
Stand up straight and authoritatively when giving your dog commands. Do not issue commands when lying on the floor or lying on your back on the sofa. If you are on your hands and knees when you give a command, your dog will think you are positioning yourself to play.

place your left hand lightly on the top of the dog's shoulders where they meet above the spinal cord. Do not push down on the dog's shoulders; simply rest your left hand there so you can guide the

your food hand at the dog's nose. Say "Stay" and step out on your right foot to stand directly in front of the dog, toe to toe, as he licks and nibbles the treat. Be sure to keep his head facing upward to maintain the sit position. Count to five and then swing around to stand next to the dog again with him on your left. As soon as you get back to the original position, release the food and praise lavishly.

To teach the down/stay, do the down as previously described. As soon as the dog lies down, say "Stay" and step out on your right foot just as you did in the sit/stay. Count to five and then return to stand beside the dog with him on your left side. Release the treat and praise as always.

Within a week or ten days, you can begin to add a bit of distance between you and your dog when you leave him. When you do, use your left hand open with the palm facing the dog as a stay signal, much the same as the hand signal a police officer uses to stop traffic at an intersection. Hold the food treat in your right hand as before, but this time the food is not touching the dog's nose. He will watch the food hand and quickly learn that he is going to get that treat as soon as you return to his side.

When you can stand 1 yard away from your dog for 30

seconds, you can then begin building time and distance in both stays. Eventually, the dog can be expected to remain in the stay position for prolonged periods of time until you return to him or call him to you. Always praise lavishly when he stays.

### TEACHING COME

If you make teaching "come" a fun experience, you should never have a student that does not love the game or that fails to come when called. The secret, it seems, is never to teach the word "come." At times when an owner most wants his dog to come when called, the owner is likely to be upset or anxious and he allows these feelings to come through in

The down-stay is an extension of the down command, requiring that the dog remain in the down position until released. Make sure the Silky doesn't feel threatened in this position and that you practice this command in a relaxed setting.

the tone of his voice when he calls his dog. Hearing that desperation in his owner's voice, the dog fears the results of going to him and therefore either disobeys outright or runs in the opposite direction. The secret, therefore, is to teach the dog a game and, when you want him to come to you, simply play the game. It is practically a no-fail solution!

To begin, have several members of your family take a few food treats and each go into a different room in the house. Take turns calling the dog, and each person should celebrate the dog's finding him with a treat and lots of happy praise. When a person calls the dog, he is actually inviting the dog to find him and get a treat as a reward for "winning."

A few turns of the "Where are you?" game and the dog will understand that everyone is playing the game and that each person has a big celebration awaiting his success at locating them. Once he learns to love the game, simply calling out "Where are you?" will bring him running from wherever he is when he hears that all-important question.

The come command is recognized as one of the most important things to teach a dog, but there are trainers who work with thousands of dogs and never teach the actual word "come." Yet these dogs will race to respond to a person who uses the dog's name followed by "Where are you?" For example, a woman has a 12-year-old companion dog who went blind, but who never fails to locate her owner when asked, "Where are you?"

Children, in particular, love to play this game with their dogs. Children can hide in smaller places like a shower or bathtub, behind a bed or under a table. The dog needs to work a little bit harder to find these hiding places but, when he does, he loves to

### "WHERE ARE YOU?"

When calling the dog, do not say "Come." Say things like, "Rover, where are you? See if you can find me! I have a biscuit for you!" Keep up a constant line of chatter with coaxing sounds and frequent questions such as, "Where are you?" The dog will learn to follow the sound of your voice to locate you and receive his reward.

celebrate with a treat and a tussle
with a favorite youngster.

### TEACHING HEEL

Heeling means that the dog walks
beside the owner without pulling.
It takes time and patience on the
owner's part to succeed at teaching the dog that he (the owner)
will not proceed unless the dog is
walking calmly beside him.
Pulling out ahead on the lead is
definitely not acceptable.

Begin by holding the lead in
your left hand as the dog sits
beside your left leg. Move the
loop end of the lead to your right
hand but keep your left hand
short on the lead so it keeps the
dog in close next to you. Say
"Heel" and step forward on your
left foot. Keep the dog close to
you and take three steps. Stop
and have the dog sit next to you
in what we now call the heel
position. Praise verbally, but do
not touch the dog. Hesitate a
moment and begin again with

**"COME" ... BACK**

Never call your dog to come to you
for a correction or scold him when he
reaches you. That is the quickest way
to turn a come command into "Go
away fast!" Dogs think only in the
present tense, and your dog will
connect the scolding with coming to
you, not with the misbehavior of a
few moments earlier.

"Heel," taking three steps and
stopping, at which point the dog
is told to sit again.

Your goal here is to have the
dog walk those three steps without pulling on the lead. Once he
will walk calmly beside you for
three steps without pulling,
increase the number of steps you
take to five. When he will walk
politely beside you while you
take five steps, you can increase
the length of your walk to ten
steps. Keep increasing the length
of your stroll until the dog will
walk quietly beside you without
pulling as long as you want him
to heel. When you stop heeling,
indicate to the dog that the exercise is over by verbally praising
as you pet him and say "OK, good

**Practice heeling
on lead in your
yard. Pet dogs and
show contenders
alike are expected
to walk on a leash
without pulling
ahead or lagging
behind.**

dog." The "OK" is used as a release word, meaning that the exercise is finished and the dog is free to relax.

If you are dealing with a dog who insists on pulling you around, simply "put on your brakes" and stand your ground until the dog realizes that the two of you are not going anywhere until he is beside you and moving at your pace, not his. It may take some time just standing there to convince the dog that you are the leader and you will be the one to decide on the direction and speed of your travel.

Each time the dog looks up at you or slows down to give a slack lead between the two of you, quietly praise him and say, "Good heel. Good dog." Eventually, the dog will begin to respond and within a few days he will be walking politely beside you without pulling on the lead. At first, the training sessions should be kept short and very positive; soon the dog will be able to walk nicely with you for increasingly longer distances. Remember also to give the dog free time and the opportunity to run and play when you have finished heel practice.

## WEANING OFF FOOD IN TRAINING

Food is used in training new behaviors. Once the dog understands what behavior goes with a specific command, it is time to start weaning him off the food treats. At first, give a treat after each exercise. Then, start to give a treat only after every other exercise. Mix up the times when you offer a food reward and the times when you only offer praise so that the dog will never know when he is going to receive both food and praise and when he is going to receive only praise. This is called a variable-ratio reward system and it proves successful because there is always the chance that the owner will produce a treat, so the dog never stops trying for that reward. No matter what, *always* give verbal praise.

## OBEDIENCE CLASSES

It is a good idea to enroll in an obedience class if one is available in your area. If yours is a show dog, handling classes would be more appropriate. Many areas have dog clubs that offer basic obedience training as well as preparatory classes for obedience competition. There are also local dog trainers who offer similar classes.

At obedience trials, dogs can earn titles at various levels of competition. The beginning levels of competition include basic behaviors such as sit, down, heel, etc. The more advanced levels of competition include jumping, retrieving, scent discrimination and signal work. The advanced levels require a dog and owner to put a lot of time and effort into

their training and the titles that can be earned at these levels of competition are very prestigious.

With the Silky's intelligence and eagerness to please, many excel in obedience competition. Don't be put off if structured training initially invites a touch of "terrier temperament." Make the experience upbeat and heap on the praise.

**OTHER ACTIVITIES FOR LIFE**
Whether a dog is trained in the structured environment of a class or alone with his owner at home, there are many activities that can bring fun and rewards to both

owner and dog once they have mastered basic control.

Teaching the dog to help out around the home, in the yard or on the farm provides great satisfaction to both dog and owner. In addition, the dog's help makes life a little easier for his owner and raises his stature as a valued companion to his family. It helps give the dog a purpose by occupying his mind and providing an outlet for his energy.

While many Silkys boast obedience titles, the sport of agility is where the breed has most fun. Racing, jumping, clearing obstacles on a timed course—agility is an event where you will see your Silky at his athletic best, doing what he loves most.

In areas where the event is available, including the US, Silkys can participate in earthdog tests—simulated ratting exercises where dogs show off their talent for tracking and burrowing after prey. Not surprisingly, this willing vermin hunter and ratter is a natural. To earn his title, the dog goes through a twisty, turning tunnel, working to beat a clock as he corners the rat (safe in a cage). To see a Silky perform is to see the true form and function of the breed. Earthdog tests are exciting competitions, great fun to watch (unless you're the rat!) and to cheer on fearless competitors. You can contact the AKC or your local dog club for details.

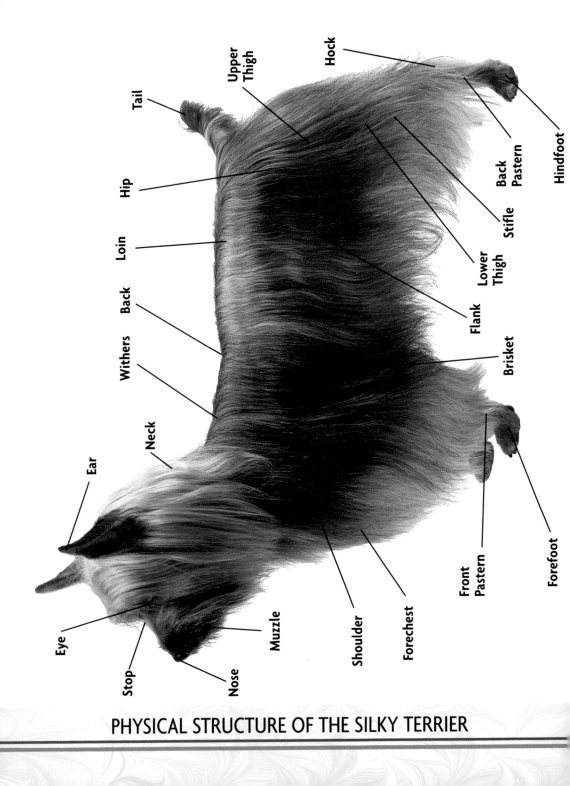

# PHYSICAL STRUCTURE OF THE SILKY TERRIER

Tail

Upper Thigh

Hock

Back Pastern

Hindfoot

Hip

Stifle

Lower Thigh

Loin

Flank

Withers

Back

Brisket

Neck

Ear

Shoulder

Forechest

Front Pastern

Forefoot

Eye

Stop

Nose

Muzzle

# SILKY TERRIER

Dogs suffer from many of the same physical illnesses as people. They might even share many of the same psychological problems. Since people usually know more about human diseases than canine maladies, many of the terms used in this chapter will be familiar but not necessarily those used by veterinarians. We will use the term *x-ray*, instead of the more acceptable term *radiograph*. We will also use the familiar term *symptoms* even though dogs don't have symptoms, which are verbal descriptions of the patient's feelings; dogs have *clinical signs*. Since dogs can't speak, we have to look for clinical signs...but we still use the term *symptoms* in this book.

As a general rule, medicine is *practiced*. That term is not arbitrary. Medicine is a constantly changing art as we learn more and more about genetics, electronic aids (like CAT scans and MRIs) and daily laboratory advances. There are many dog maladies, like canine hip dysplasia, which are not universally treated in the same manner. Some vets opt for surgery more often than others do.

## SELECTING A QUALIFIED VET

Your selection of a veterinarian should be based upon recommendations, personality and skills as well as upon convenience to your home. You want a vet who is close because you might have emergencies or need to make multiple visits for treatments. You want a vet who has services that you might require such as tattooing and boarding facilities, and of course a good reputation for ability and responsiveness. There is nothing more frustrating than having to wait a day or more to get a response from your vet.

All vets are licensed and should be capable of dealing with routine health issues and promotion of health. Most vets do routine surgery such as neutering, stitching up wounds and docking tails for those breeds in which such is required for show purposes. There are, however, many veterinary specialties that require further studies and internships. These include specialists in heart problems (veterinary cardiologists), skin problems (veterinary dermatologists), teeth and gum problems (veterinary

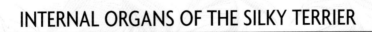

1. Esophagus
2. Lungs
3. Gall Bladder
4. Liver
5. Kidney
6. Stomach
7. Intestines
8. Urinary Bladder

# INTERNAL ORGANS OF THE SILKY TERRIER

dentists), eye problems (veterinary ophthalmologists) and x-rays (veterinary radiologists), as well as vets who have specialties in bones, muscles or certain organs.

When the problem affecting your dog is serious, it is not unusual or impudent to get another medical opinion, although it is wise and courteous to advise the vets concerned about this. You might also want to compare costs among several veterinarians. Sophisticated health care and veterinary services can be very costly. It is not infrequent that important decisions are based upon financial considerations.

## PREVENTATIVE MEDICINE

It is much easier, less costly and more effective to practice preventative medicine than to fight bouts of illness and disease. Properly bred puppies come from parents who were selected based upon their genetic-disease profiles. Their mother should have been vaccinated, free of all internal and external parasites and properly nourished. For these reasons, a visit to the vet who cared for the dam is recommended. The dam can pass on disease resistance to her puppies, which can last for eight to ten weeks. She can also pass on parasites and many infections. That's why you should learn as much about the dam's health as possible.

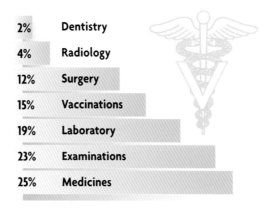

**Breakdown of Veterinary Income by Category**

| | |
|---|---|
| 2% | Dentistry |
| 4% | Radiology |
| 12% | Surgery |
| 15% | Vaccinations |
| 19% | Laboratory |
| 23% | Examinations |
| 25% | Medicines |

A typical vet's income, categorized according to services performed. This survey dealt with small-animal (pets) practices.

**WEANING TO BRINGING PUP HOME**
Puppies should be weaned by the time they are about two months old. A puppy that remains for at least eight weeks with his dam and littermates usually adapts better to other dogs and people later in life.

Sometimes new owners have their puppy examined by a veterinarian immediately, which is a good idea unless the pup is tired from the journey home. In that case, an appointment should be made for the next day.

The puppy will have his teeth examined and his skeletal conformation and general health checked prior to certification by the vet. Puppies of certain breeds can have problems with their kneecaps, undescended testicles, cataracts and other eye problems and heart murmurs. Your vet might have training in temperament evaluation.

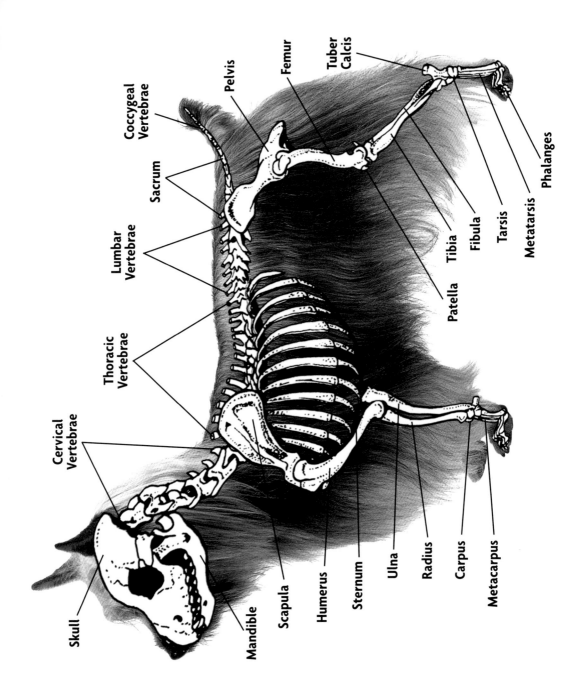

Coccygeal Vertebrae
Pelvis
Femur
Tuber Calcis
Sacrum
Lumbar Vertebrae
Thoracic Vertebrae
Patella
Tibia
Fibula
Tarsis
Metatarsis
Phalanges
Cervical Vertebrae
Skull
Mandible
Scapula
Humerus
Sternum
Ulna
Radius
Carpus
Metacarpus

# SKELETAL STRUCTURE OF THE SILKY TERRIER

At the first visit your vet will schedule your pup's vaccinations.

VACCINATION SCHEDULING
Most vaccinations are given by injection and should only be done by a vet. From the onset of your relationship with your vet, be sure to advise him that Silky Terriers can be particularly sensitive to inoculations and other injections. Both he and you should keep a record of the date of the injection, the identification of the vaccine and the amount given. Some vets give a first vaccination at six weeks, but most dog breeders prefer the course not to commence until about eight weeks because of negating any antibodies passed on by the dam. The vaccination scheduling is usually based on a two- to four-week cycle. You must take your vet's advice regarding when to vaccinate, as this may differ according to the vaccine used.

Most vaccinations immunize your puppy against viruses. The usual vaccines contain immunizing doses of several different viruses such as distemper, parvovirus, parainfluenza and hepatitis although some veterinarians recommend separate vaccines for each disease. There are other

# HEALTH AND VACCINATION SCHEDULE

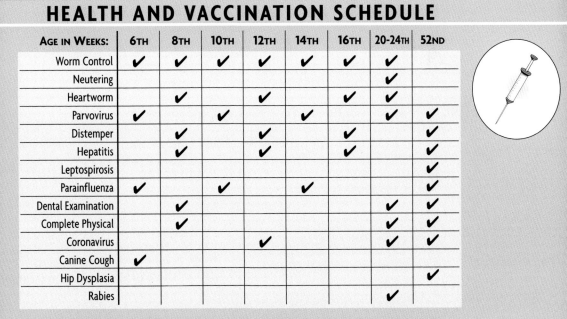

| AGE IN WEEKS: | 6TH | 8TH | 10TH | 12TH | 14TH | 16TH | 20-24TH | 52ND |
|---|---|---|---|---|---|---|---|---|
| Worm Control | ✔ | ✔ | ✔ | ✔ | ✔ | ✔ | ✔ | |
| Neutering | | | | | | | ✔ | |
| Heartworm | | ✔ | | ✔ | | ✔ | ✔ | |
| Parvovirus | ✔ | | ✔ | | ✔ | | ✔ | ✔ |
| Distemper | | ✔ | | ✔ | | ✔ | | ✔ |
| Hepatitis | | ✔ | | ✔ | | ✔ | | ✔ |
| Leptospirosis | | | | | | | | ✔ |
| Parainfluenza | ✔ | | ✔ | | ✔ | | | ✔ |
| Dental Examination | | ✔ | | | | | ✔ | ✔ |
| Complete Physical | | ✔ | | | | | ✔ | ✔ |
| Coronavirus | | | | ✔ | | | ✔ | ✔ |
| Canine Cough | ✔ | | | | | | | |
| Hip Dysplasia | | | | | | | | ✔ |
| Rabies | | | | | | | ✔ | |

Vaccinations are not instantly effective. It takes about two weeks for the dog's immune system to develop antibodies. Most vaccinations require annual booster shots. Your vet should guide you in this regard.

vaccines available when the puppy is at risk. You should rely upon professional advice. This is especially true for the booster-shot program. Most vaccination programs require a booster when the puppy is a year old and once a year thereafter. In some cases, circumstances may require more or less frequent immunizations. Canine cough, more formally known as tracheobronchitis, is treated with a vaccine that is sprayed into the dog's nostrils.

Canine cough is usually included in routine vaccination, but this is often not so effective as for other major diseases.

### FIVE TO TWELVE MONTHS OF AGE

Unless you intend to breed or show your dog, neutering the puppy around six months of age is recommended. Discuss this with your vet. Neutering/spaying has proven to be extremely beneficial to both male and female dogs. Besides eliminating the possibility

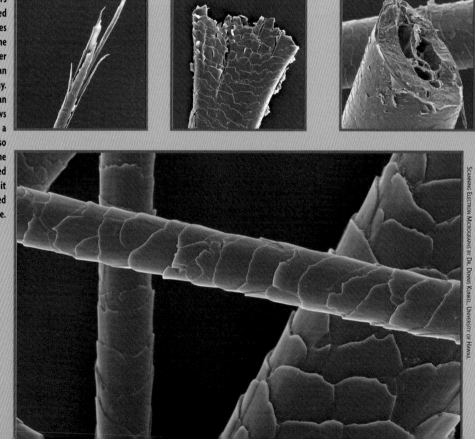

Normal hairs of a dog enlarged 200 times original size. The cuticle (outer covering) is clean and healthy. Unlike human hair that grows from the base, a dog's hair also grows from the end. Damaged hairs and split ends, illustrated above.

SCANNING ELECTRON MICROGRAPHS BY DR. DENNIS KUNKEL, UNIVERSITY OF HAWAII.

# DISEASE REFERENCE CHART

| | What is it? | What causes it? | Symptoms |
|---|---|---|---|
| **Leptospirosis** | Severe disease that affects the internal organs; can be spread to people. | A bacterium, which is often carried by rodents, that enters through mucous membranes and spreads quickly throughout the body. | Range from fever, vomiting and loss of appetite in less severe cases to shock, irreversible kidney damage and possibly death in most severe cases. |
| **Rabies** | Potentially deadly virus that infects warm-blooded mammals. | Bite from a carrier of the virus, mainly wild animals. | 1st stage: dog exhibits change in behavior, fear. 2nd stage: dog's behavior becomes more aggressive. 3rd stage: loss of coordination, trouble with bodily functions. |
| **Parvovirus** | Highly contagious virus, potentially deadly. | Ingestion of the virus, which is usually spread through the feces of infected dogs. | Most common: severe diarrhea. Also vomiting, fatigue, lack of appetite. |
| **Canine cough** | Contagious respiratory infection. | Combination of types of bacteria and virus. Most common: *Bordetella bronchiseptica* bacteria and parainfluenza virus. | Chronic cough. |
| **Distemper** | Disease primarily affecting respiratory and nervous system. | Virus that is related to the human measles virus. | Mild symptoms such as fever, lack of appetite and mucus secretion progress to evidence of brain damage, "hard pad." |
| **Hepatitis** | Virus primarily affecting the liver. | Canine adenovirus type I (CAV-1). Enters system when dog breathes in particles. | Lesser symptoms include listlessness, diarrhea, vomiting. More severe symptoms include "blue-eye" (clumps of virus in eye). |
| **Coronavirus** | Virus resulting in digestive problems. | Virus is spread through infected dog's feces. | Stomach upset evidenced by lack of appetite, vomiting, diarrhea. |

of pregnancy and pyometra in bitches and testicular cancer in males, it greatly reduces the risk of breast cancer in bitches and prostate cancer in males.

Your vet should provide your puppy with a thorough dental evaluation at six months of age, ascertaining whether all of the permanent teeth have erupted properly. A home dental-care regimen should be initiated at six months, including brushing weekly and providing good dental

devices (such as nylon bones). Regular dental care promotes healthy teeth, fresh breath and a longer life.

### OLDER THAN ONE YEAR

Once a year, your full-grown dog should visit the vet for an examination and vaccination boosters, if needed. Some vets recommend blood tests, thyroid level check and dental evaluation to accompany these annual visits. A thorough clinical evaluation by the vet

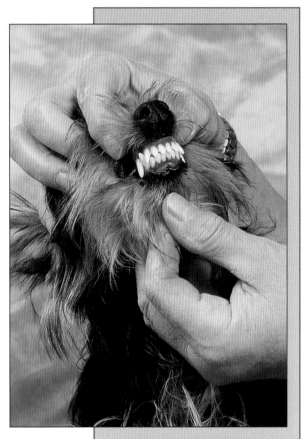

**CARETAKER OF TEETH**
You are your dog's caretaker and his dentist. Vets warn that plaque and tartar buildup on the teeth will damage the gums and allow bacteria to enter the dog's bloodstream, causing serious damage to the animal's vital organs. Studies show that over 50 percent of dogs have some form of gum disease before age three. Daily or weekly tooth cleaning (with a brush or soft gauze pad wipes) can add to your dog's life.

can provide critical background information for your dog. Blood tests are often performed at one year of age, and dental examinations should be part of your dog's check-ups. In the long run, quality preventative care for your pet can improve and prolong his life.

**SKIN PROBLEMS**
Veterinarians are consulted by dog owners for skin problems more than any other group of diseases or maladies. Dogs' skin is almost as sensitive as human skin and both can suffer from almost the same ailments (though the occurrence of acne in most dogs is rare). For this reason, veterinary dermatology has developed into a specialty practiced by many veterinarians.

Since many skin problems have visual symptoms that are almost identical, it requires the skill of an experienced veterinary dermatologist to identify and cure many of the more severe skin disorders. Pet shops sell many treatments for skin problems, but most of the treatments are directed at symptoms and not the underlying problem(s). If your dog is suffering from a skin disorder, you should seek professional assistance as quickly as possible. As with all diseases, the earlier a problem is identified and treated, the more likely is a complete cure.

## HEREDITARY SKIN DISORDERS

Veterinary dermatologists are currently researching a number of skin disorders that are believed to have a hereditary basis. These inherited diseases are transmitted by both parents, who appear (phenotypically) normal but have a recessive gene for the disease, meaning that they carry, but are not affected by, the disease. These diseases pose serious problems to breeders because in some instances there is no method of identifying carriers. Often the secondary diseases associated with these skin conditions are even more debilitating than the disorder itself, including cancers and respiratory problems.

Among the hereditary skin disorders, for which the mode of inheritance is known, are: acrodermatitis, cutaneous asthenia (Ehlers-Danlos syndrome), sebaceous adenitis, cyclic hematopoiesis, dermatomyositis, IgA deficiency, color dilution alopecia and nodular dermatofibrosis. Some of these disorders are limited to one or two breeds and others affect a large number of breeds. All inherited diseases must be diagnosed and treated by a veterinary specialist.

## PARASITE BITES

Many of us are allergic to insect bites. The bites itch, erupt and may even become infected. Dogs

**KNOW WHEN TO POSTPONE A VACCINATION**
While the visit to the vet is costly, it is never advisable to update a vaccination when visiting with a sick or pregnant dog. Vaccinations should be avoided for all elderly dogs. If your dog is showing the signs of any illness or any medical condition, no matter how serious or mild, including skin irritations, do not vaccinate. Likewise, a lame dog should never be vaccinated; any dog undergoing surgery or on any immunosuppressant drugs should not be vaccinated until fully recovered.

## VITAL SIGNS

A dog's normal temperature is 101.5 degrees Fahrenheit. A range of between 100.0 and 102.5 degrees should be considered normal, as each dog's body sets its own temperature. It will be helpful if you take your dog's temperature when you know he is healthy and record it. Then, when you suspect that he is not feeling well, you will have a normal figure to compare the abnormal temperature against.

The normal pulse rate for a dog is between 100 and 125 beats per minute.

have the same reaction to fleas, ticks and/or mites. When an insect lands on you, you have the chance to whisk it away with your hand. Unfortunately, when your dog is bitten by a flea, tick or mite, he can only scratch it away or bite it. By the time the dog has been bitten, the parasite has done some of its damage. It may also have laid eggs to cause further problems in the near future. The itching from parasite bites is probably due to the saliva injected into the site when the parasite sucks the dog's blood.

AUTO-IMMUNE SKIN CONDITIONS
Auto-immune skin conditions are commonly referred to as being allergic to yourself, while allergies are usually inflammatory reactions to an outside stimulus. Auto-immune diseases cause serious damage to the tissues that are involved.

The best known auto-immune disease is lupus, which affects people as well as dogs. The symptoms are variable and may affect the kidneys, bones, blood chemistry and skin. It can be fatal to both dogs and humans, though it is not thought to be transmissible. It is usually successfully treated with cortisone, prednisone or a similar corticosteroid, but extensive use of these drugs can have harmful side effects.

### THE SAME ALLERGIES
Chances are that you and your dog will have the same allergies. Your allergies are readily recognizable and usually easily treated. Your dog's allergies may be masked.

## AIRBORNE ALLERGIES

Just as humans have hay fever, rose fever and other fevers from which we suffer during the pollinating season, many dogs suffer the same allergies. When the pollen count is high, your dog might suffer, but don't expect him to sneeze and have a runny nose like a human would. Dogs react to pollen allergies the same way they react to fleas—they scratch and bite themselves.

Dogs, like humans, can be tested for allergens. Discuss the testing with your veterinary dermatologist.

## FOOD PROBLEMS

### FOOD ALLERGIES

Dogs are allergic to many foods that are best-sellers and highly recommended by breeders and vets. Changing the brand of food that you buy may not eliminate the problem if the element to which the dog is allergic is also contained in the new brand.

Recognizing a food allergy is difficult. Humans vomit or have rashes when we eat a food to which we are allergic. Dogs neither vomit nor (usually) develop a rash. They react in the same manner as they do to an airborne or flea allergy; they itch, scratch and bite, thus making the diagnosis extremely difficult. While pollen allergies and parasite bites are usually seasonal, food allergies are year-round problems.

### FOOD INTOLERANCE

Food intolerance is the inability of the dog to completely digest certain foods. For example, puppies that may have done very well on their mother's milk may not do well on cow's milk. The result of this food intolerance may be loose bowels, passing gas and stomach pains. These are the only obvious symptoms of food

Your veterinarian can demonstrate for you how to administer oral medications to your dog.

intolerance and that makes diagnosis difficult.

### TREATING FOOD PROBLEMS

It is possible to handle food allergies and food intolerance yourself. Put your dog on a diet that he has never had.

**PROPER DIET**

Feeding your dog properly is very important. An incorrect diet could affect the dog's health, behavior and nervous system, possibly making a normal dog into an aggressive one. Its most visible effects are to the skin and coat, but internal organs are similarly affected.

Obviously, if he has never eaten this new food, he can't yet have been allergic or intolerant of it. Start with a single ingredient that is not in the dog's diet at the present time. Ingredients like chopped beef or chicken are common in dogs' diets, so try something different like fish, lamb or some other quality source of protein. Keep the dog on this diet (with no additives) for a month. If the symptoms of food allergy or intolerance disappear, chances are your dog has a food allergy.

Don't think that the single ingredient cured the problem. You still must find a suitable diet and ascertain which ingredient in the old diet was objectionable. This is most easily done by adding ingredients to the new diet one at a time. Let the dog stay on the modified diet for a month before you add another ingredient. Eventually, you will determine the ingredient that caused the adverse reaction.

An alternative method is to carefully study the ingredients in the diet to which your dog is allergic or intolerant. Identify the main ingredient in this diet and eliminate the main ingredient by buying a different food that does not have that ingredient. Keep experimenting until the symptoms disappear after one month on the new diet.

# Number-One Killer Disease in Dogs: CANCER

In every age, there is a word associated with a disease or plague that causes humans to shudder. In the 21st century, that word is "cancer." Just as cancer is the leading cause of death in humans, it claims nearly half the lives of dogs that die from a natural disease as well as half the dogs that die over the age of ten years.

Described as a genetic disease, cancer becomes a greater risk as the dog ages. Vets and dog owners have become increasingly aware of the threat of cancer to dogs. Statistics reveal that one dog in every five will develop cancer, the most common of which is skin cancer. Many cancers, including prostate, ovarian and breast cancer, can be avoided by spaying and neutering our dogs by the age of six months.

Early detection of cancer can save or extend a dog's life, so it is absolutely vital for owners to have their dogs examined by a qualified vet or oncologist immediately upon detection of any abnormality. Certain dietary guidelines have also proven to reduce the onset and spread of cancer. Foods based on fish rather than beef, due to the presence of Omega-3 fatty acids, are recommended. Other amino acids such as glutamine have significant benefits for canines, particularly those breeds that show a greater susceptibility to cancer.

Cancer management and treatments promise hope for future generations of canines. Since the disease is genetic, breeders should never breed a dog whose parents, grandparents and any related siblings have developed cancer. It is difficult to know whether to exclude an otherwise healthy dog from a breeding program, as the disease does not manifest itself until the dog's senior years.

## RECOGNIZE CANCER WARNING SIGNS

Since early detection can possibly rescue your dog from becoming a cancer statistic, it is essential for owners to recognize the possible signs and seek the assistance of a qualified professional.

- Abnormal bumps or lumps that continue to grow
- Bleeding or discharge from any body cavity
- Persistent stiffness or lameness
- Recurrent sores or sores that do not heal
- Inappetence
- Breathing difficulties
- Weight loss
- Bad breath or odors
- General malaise and fatigue
- Eating and swallowing problems
- Difficulty urinating and defecating

| Disease | % |
|---|---|
| Cancer | 47% |
| Heart disease | 12% |
| Kidney disease | 7% |
| Epilepsy | 4% |
| Liver disease | 4% |
| Bloat | 3% |
| Diabetes | 3% |
| Stroke | 2% |
| Cushing's disease | 2% |
| Immune diseases | 2% |
| Other causes | 14% |

**The Ten Most Common Fatal Diseases in Pure-bred Dogs**

A male dog flea, *Ctenocephalides canis.*

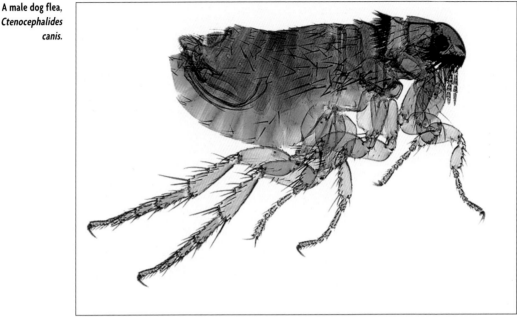

Photo by Jean Claude Revy/Phototake.

## EXTERNAL PARASITES

### FLEAS

Of all the problems to which dogs are prone, none is more well known and frustrating than fleas. Flea infestation is relatively simple to cure but difficult to prevent. Parasites that are harbored inside the body are a bit more difficult to eradicate but they are easier to control.

To control flea infestation, you have to understand the flea's life cycle. Fleas are often thought of as a summertime problem, but centrally heated homes have changed the patterns and fleas can be found at any time of the year. The most effective method of flea control is a two-stage approach: one stage to kill the adult fleas, and the other to control the development of pre-adult fleas. Unfortunately, no single active ingredient is effective against all stages of the life cycle.

### FLEA KILLER CAUTION—"POISON"

Flea-killers are poisonous. You should not spray these toxic chemicals on areas of a dog's body that he licks, including his genitals and his face. Flea killers taken internally are a better answer, but check with your vet in case internal therapy is not advised for your dog.

## LIFE CYCLE STAGES

During its life, a flea will pass through four life stages: egg, larva, pupa or nymph and adult. The adult stage is the most visible and irritating stage of the flea life cycle, and this is why the majority of flea-control products concentrate on this stage. The fact is that adult fleas account for only 1% of the total flea population, and the other 99% exist in pre-adult stages, i.e., eggs, larvae and nymphs. The pre-adult stages are barely visible to the naked eye.

## THE LIFE CYCLE OF THE FLEA

Eggs are laid on the dog, usually in quantities of about 20 or 30, several times a day. The adult female flea must have a blood meal before each egg-laying session. When first laid, the eggs will cling to the dog's hair, as the eggs are still moist. However, they will quickly dry out and fall from the dog, especially if the dog moves around or scratches. Many eggs will fall off in the dog's favorite area or an area in which he spends a lot of time, such as his bed.

Once the eggs fall from the dog onto the carpet or furniture, they will hatch into larvae. This takes from one to ten days. Larvae are not particularly mobile and will usually travel only a few inches from where they hatch. However, they do have a tendency to move away from bright light and heavy

**EN GARDE:**
**CATCHING FLEAS OFF GUARD!**
Consider the following ways to arm yourself against fleas:
- Add a small amount of pennyroyal or eucalyptus oil to your dog's bath. These natural remedies repel fleas.
- Supplement your dog's food with fresh garlic (minced or grated) and a hearty amount of brewer's yeast, both of which ward off fleas.
- Use a flea comb on your dog daily. Submerge fleas in a cup of bleach to kill them quickly.
- Confine the dog to only a few rooms to limit the spread of fleas in the home.
- Vacuum daily...and get all of the crevices! Dispose of the bag every few days until the problem is under control.
- Wash your dog's bedding daily. Cover cushions where your dog sleeps with towels, and wash the towels often.

traffic—under furniture and behind doors are common places to find high quantities of flea larvae.

The flea larvae feed on dead organic matter, including adult flea feces, until they are ready to change into adult fleas. Fleas will usually remain as larvae for around seven days. After this period, the larvae will pupate into protective pupae. While inside the pupae, the larvae will undergo metamorphosis and change into

PHOTO BY DWIGHT R. KUHN.

**Fleas have been measured as being able to jump 300,000 times and can jump over 150 times their length in any direction, including straight up.**

adult fleas. This can take as little time as a few days, but the adult fleas can remain inside the pupae waiting to hatch for up to two years. The pupae are signaled to hatch by certain stimuli, such as physical pressure—the pupae's being stepped on, heat from an animal's lying on the pupae or increased carbon-dioxide levels and vibrations—indicating that a suitable host is available.

Once hatched, the adult flea must feed within a few days. Once the adult flea finds a host, it will not leave voluntarily. It only becomes dislodged by grooming or the host animal's scratching. The adult flea will remain on the

host for the duration of its life unless forcibly removed.

### TREATING THE ENVIRONMENT AND THE DOG

Treating fleas should be a two-pronged attack. First, the environment needs to be treated; this includes carpets and furniture, especially the dog's bedding and areas underneath furniture. The environment should be treated with a household spray containing an Insect Growth Regulator (IGR) and an insecticide to kill the adult fleas. Most IGRs are effective against eggs and larvae; they actually mimic the fleas' own hormones and stop the eggs and larvae from developing into adult fleas. There are currently no treatments available to attack the pupa stage of the life cycle, so the adult insecticide is used to kill the newly hatched adult fleas before they find a host. Most IGRs are active for many months, while adult insecticides are only active for a few days.

**A scanning electron micrograph of a dog or cat flea, *Ctenocephalides*, magnified more than 100x. This image has been colorized for effect.**

S. E. M. BY DR DENNIS KUNKEL, UNIVERSITY OF HAWAII.

# THE LIFE CYCLE OF THE FLEA

**Adult**

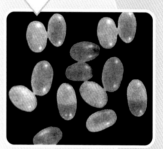

**Egg**

**Pupa
or
Nymph**

**Larva**

Fleas have been around for millions of years and have adapted to changing host animals. They are able to go through a complete life cycle in less than one month or they can extend their lives to almost two years by remaining as pupae or cocoons. They do not need blood or any other food for up to 20 months.

## INSECT GROWTH REGULATOR (IGR)

Two types of products should be used when treating fleas—a product to treat the pet and a product to treat the home. Adult fleas represent less than 1% of the flea population. The pre-adult fleas (eggs, larvae and pupae) represent more than 99% of the flea population and are found in the environment; it is in the case of pre-adult fleas that products containing an Insect Growth Regulator (IGR) should be used in the home.

IGRs are a new class of compounds used to prevent the development of insects. They do not kill the insect outright, but instead use the insect's biology against it to stop it from completing its growth. Products that contain methoprene are the world's first and leading IGRs. Used to control fleas and other insects, this type of IGR will stop flea larvae from developing and protect the house for up to seven months.

*The American dog tick,* Dermacentor variabilis, *is probably the most common tick found on dogs. Look at the strength in its eight legs! No wonder it's hard to detach them.*

When treating with a household spray, it is a good idea to vacuum before applying the product. This stimulates as many pupae as possible to hatch into adult fleas. The vacuum cleaner should also be treated with an insecticide to prevent the eggs and larvae that have been collected in the vacuum bag from hatching.

The second stage of treatment is to apply an adult insecticide to the dog. Traditionally, this would be in the form of a collar or a spray, but more recent innovations include digestible insecticides that poison the fleas when they ingest the dog's blood. Alternatively, there are drops that, when placed on the back of the dog's neck, spread throughout the hair and skin to kill adult fleas.

### TICKS

Though not as common as fleas, ticks are found all over the tropical and temperate world. They don't bite, like fleas; they harpoon. They dig their sharp proboscis (nose) into the dog's skin and drink the blood. Their only food and drink is dog's blood. Dogs can get Lyme

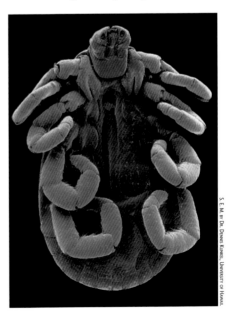

disease, Rocky Mountain spotted fever, tick bite paralysis and many other diseases from ticks. They may live where fleas are found and they like to hide in cracks or seams in walls. They are controlled the same way fleas are controlled.

The American dog tick, *Dermacentor variabilis*, may well be the most common dog tick in many geographical areas, especially those areas where the climate is hot and humid. Most dog ticks have life expectancies of a week to six months, depending upon climatic conditions. They can neither jump nor fly, but they can crawl slowly and can range up to 16 feet to reach a sleeping or unsuspecting dog.

## MITES

Just as fleas and ticks can be problematic for your dog, mites can also lead to an itchy nuisance. Microscopic in size, mites are related to ticks and generally take up permanent residence on their host animal— in this case, your dog! The term *mange* refers to any infestation caused by one of the mighty mites, of which there are six varieties that concern dog owners.

*Demodex* mites cause a condition known as demodicosis (sometimes called red mange or follicular mange), in which the

**DEER-TICK CROSSING**
The great outdoors may be fun for your dog, but it also is a home to dangerous ticks. Deer ticks carry a bacterium known as *Borrelia burgdorferi* and are most active in the autumn and spring. When infections are caught early, penicillin and tetracycline are effective antibiotics, but, if left untreated, the bacteria may cause neurological, kidney and cardiac problems as well as long-term trouble with walking and painful joints.

S. E. M. BY DR. ANDREW SPIELMAN/PHOTOTAKE.

PHOTO BY DR. DENNIS KUNKEL, UNIVERSITY OF HAWAII.

The head of an American dog tick, *Dermacentor variabilis*, enlarged and colorized for effect.

The mange mite, *Psoroptes bovis*, can infest cattle and other domestic animals.

Photo by James Hayden/Yown/Phototake.

mites live in the dog's hair follicles and sebaceous glands in larger-than-normal numbers. This type of mange is commonly passed from the dam to her puppies and usually shows up on the puppies' muzzles, though demodicosis is not transferable from one normal dog to another. Most dogs recover from this type of mange without any treatment, though topical therapies are commonly prescribed by the vet.

Human lice look like dog lice; the two are closely related.

Photo by Dwight R. Kuhn.

The *Cheyletiellosis* mite is the hook-mouthed culprit associated with "walking dandruff," a condition that affects dogs as well as cats and rabbits. This mite lives on the surface of the animal's skin and is readily transferable through direct or indirect contact with an affected animal. The dandruff is present in the form of scaly skin, which may or may not be itchy. If not treated, this mange can affect a whole kennel of dogs and can be spread to humans as well.

The *Sarcoptes* mite causes intense itching on the dog in the form of a condition known as scabies or sarcoptic mange. The cycle of the *Sarcoptes* mite lasts about three weeks, and the mites live in the top layer of the dog's skin (epidermis), preferably in areas with little hair. Scabies is highly contagious and can be passed to humans. Sometimes an allergic reaction to the mite worsens the severe itching associated with sarcoptic mange.

Ear mites, *Otodectes cynotis,* lead to otodectic mange, which most commonly affects the outer ear canal of the dog, though other areas can be affected as well. Dogs with ear-mite infestation commonly scratch at their ears, causing further irritation, and shake their heads. Dark brown droppings in the outer ear confirm the diagnosis. Your vet can prescribe a treatment to flush out the ears and kill any eggs in the ears. A complete month of treatment is necessary to cure the mange.

Two other mites, less common in dogs, include *Dermanyssus gallinae* (the poultry or red mite) and *Eutrombicula alfreddugesi* (the North American mite associated with trombiculidiasis or chigger infestation). The poultry mite frequently lives on chickens, but can transfer to dogs who spend time near farm animals. Chigger infestation affects dogs in the Central US who

**NOT A DROP TO DRINK**
Never allow your dog to swim in polluted water or public areas where water quality can be suspect. Even perfectly clear water can harbor parasites, many of which can cause serious to fatal illnesses in canines. Areas inhabited by waterfowl and other wildlife are especially dangerous.

have exposure to woodlands. The types of mange caused by both of these mites are treatable by vets.

**INTERNAL PARASITES**
Most animals—fishes, birds and mammals, including dogs and humans—have worms and other parasites that live inside their bodies. According to Dr. Herbert R. Axelrod, the fish pathologist, there are two kinds of parasites: dumb and smart. The smart parasites live in peaceful cooperation with their hosts (symbiosis), while the dumb parasites kill their hosts. Most worm infections are relatively easy to control. If they are not controlled, they weaken the host dog to the point that other medical problems occur, but they do not kill the host as dumb parasites would.

The brown dog tick, *Rhipicephalus sanguineus*, is an uncommon but annoying tick found on dogs.
PHOTO BY CAROLINA BIOLOGICAL SUPPLY/PHOTOTAKE.

**DO NOT MIX**
Never mix parasite-control products without first consulting your vet. Some products can become toxic when combined with others and can cause fatal consequences.

The roundworm *Rhabditis* can infect both dogs and humans.

## ROUNDWORMS

Average-size dogs can pass 1,360,000 roundworm eggs every day. For example, if there were only 1 million dogs in the world, the world would be saturated with thousands of tons of dog feces. These feces would contain around 15,000,000,000 roundworm eggs.

Up to 31% of home yards and children's sand boxes in the US contain roundworm eggs.

Flushing dog's feces down the toilet is not a safe practice because the usual sewage treatments do not destroy roundworm eggs.

Infected puppies start shedding roundworm eggs at three weeks of age. They can be infected by their mother's milk.

The roundworm, *Ascaris lumbricoides.*

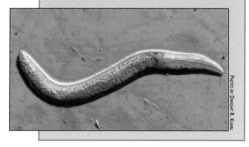

## ROUNDWORMS

The roundworms that infect dogs are known scientifically as *Toxocara canis*. They live in the dog's intestines and shed eggs continually. It has been estimated that a dog produces about 6 or more ounces of feces every day. Each ounce of feces averages hundreds of thousands of roundworm eggs. There are no known areas in which dogs roam that do not contain roundworm eggs. The greatest danger of roundworms is that they infect people, too! It is wise to have your dog tested regularly for roundworms.

In young puppies, roundworms cause bloated bellies, diarrhea, coughing and vomiting, and are transmitted from the dam (through blood or milk). Affected puppies will not appear as animated as normal puppies. The worms appear spaghetti-like, measuring as long as 6 inches. Adult dogs can acquire roundworms through coprophagia (eating contaminated feces) or by killing rodents that carry roundworms.

Roundworm infection can kill puppies and cause severe problems in adults, as the hatched larvae travel to the lungs and trachea through the bloodstream. Cleanliness is the best preventative for roundworms. Always pick up after your dog and dispose of feces in appropriate receptacles.

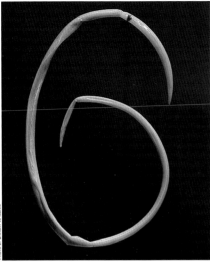

The hookworm, *Ancylostoma caninum.*

## HOOKWORMS

In the United States, dog owners have to be concerned about four different species of hookworm, the most common and most serious of which is *Ancylostoma caninum,* which prefers warm climates. The others are *Ancylostoma braziliense, Ancylostoma tubaeforme* and *Uncinaria stenocephala,* the latter of which is a concern to dogs living in the Northern US and Canada, as this species prefers cold climates. Hookworms are dangerous to humans as well as to dogs and cats, and can be the cause of severe anemia due to iron deficiency. The worm uses its teeth to attach itself to the dog's intestines and changes the site of its attachment about six times per day. Each time the worm repositions itself, the dog loses blood and can become anemic. *Ancylostoma caninum* is the most likely of the four species to cause anemia in the dog.

Symptoms of hookworm infection include dark stools, weight loss, general weakness, pale coloration and anemia, as well as possible skin problems. Fortunately, hookworms are easily purged from the affected dog with a number of medications that have proven effective. Discuss these with your vet. Most heartworm preventatives include a hookworm insecticide as well.

Owners also must be aware that hookworms can infect humans, who can acquire the larvae through exposure to contaminated feces. Since the worms cannot complete their life cycle on a human, the worms simply infest the skin and cause irritation. This condition is known as cutaneous larva migrans syndrome. As a preventative, use disposable gloves or a "poop-scoop" to pick up your dog's droppings and prevent your dog (or neighborhood cats) from defecating in children's play areas.

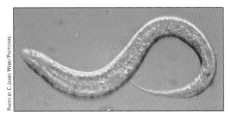

The infective stage of the hookworm larva.

## TAPEWORMS

Humans, rats, squirrels, foxes, coyotes, wolves and domestic dogs are all susceptible to tapeworm infection. Except in humans, tapeworms are usually not a fatal infection. Infected individuals can harbor 1000 parasitic worms.

Tapeworms, like some other types of worm, are hermaphroditic, meaning male and female in the same worm.

If dogs eat infected rats or mice, or anything else infected with tapeworm, they get the tapeworm disease. One month after attaching to a dog's intestine, the worm starts shedding eggs. These eggs are infective immediately. Infective eggs can live for a few months without a host animal.

The head and rostellum (the round prominence on the scolex) of a tapeworm, which infects dogs and humans.

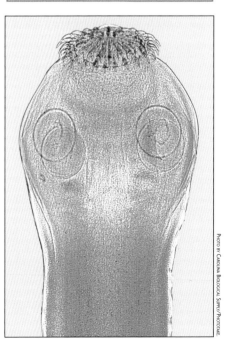

PHOTO BY CAROLINA BIOLOGICAL SUPPLY/PHOTOTAKE

## TAPEWORMS

There are many species of tapeworm, all of which are carried by fleas! The most common tapeworm affecting dogs is known as *Dipylidium caninum*. The dog eats the flea and starts the tapeworm cycle. Humans can also be infected with tapeworms—so don't eat fleas! Fleas are so small that your dog could pass them onto your hands, your plate or your food and thus make it possible for you to ingest a flea that is carrying tapeworm eggs.

While tapeworm infection is not life-threatening in dogs (smart parasite!), it can be the cause of a very serious liver disease for humans. About 50% of the humans infected with *Echinococcus multilocularis*, a type of tapeworm that causes alveolar hydatid, perish.

## WHIPWORMS

In North America, whipworms are counted among the most common parasitic worms in dogs. The whipworm's scientific name is *Trichuris vulpis*. These worms attach themselves in the lower parts of the intestine, where they feed. Affected dogs may only experience upset tummies, colic and diarrhea. These worms, however, can live for months or years in the dog, beginning their larval stage in the small intestine, spending their adult stage in the large intestine and finally passing infective eggs through the dog's feces. The only way to detect whipworms is through a fecal examination, though this is not always foolproof. Treatment for whipworms is tricky, due to the worms' unusual life-cycle pattern, and very often dogs are reinfected due to exposure to infective eggs on the ground. The whipworm eggs can survive in the environment for as long as five years; thus, cleaning up droppings in your own backyard as well as in public places is absolutely essential for sanitation purposes and the health of your dog and others.

### THREADWORMS

Though less common than roundworms, hookworms and those previously mentioned, thread-worms concern dog owners in the Southwestern US and Gulf Coast area where the climate is hot and humid. Living in the small intestine of the dog, this worm measures a mere 2 millimeters and is round in shape. Like that of the whipworm, the threadworm's life cycle is very complex and the eggs and larvae are passed through the feces. A deadly disease in humans, *Strongyloides* readily infects people, and the handling of feces is the most common means of transmission. Threadworms are most often seen in young puppies; bloody diarrhea and pneumonia are symptoms. Sick puppies must be isolated and treated immediately; vets recommend a follow-up treatment one month later.

## HEARTWORM PREVENTATIVES

There are many heartworm preventatives on the market, many of which are sold at your veterinarian's office. These products can be given daily or monthly, depending on the manufacturer's instructions. All of these preventatives contain chemical insecticides directed at killing heartworms, which leads to some controversy among dog owners. In effect, heartworm preventatives are necessary evils, though you should determine how necessary based on your pet's lifestyle. There is no doubt that heartworm is a dreadful disease that threatens the lives of dogs. However, the likelihood of your dog's being bitten by an infected mosquito is slim in most places, and a mosquito-repellent (or an herbal remedy such as Wormwood or Black Walnut) is much safer for your dog and will not compromise his immune system (the way heartworm preventatives will). Should you decide to use the traditional preventative "medications," you can consider giving the pill every other or third month. Since the toxins in the pill will kill the heartworms at all stages of development, the pill would be effective in killing larvae, nymphs or adults, and it takes four months for the larvae to reach the adult stage. Thus, there is no rationale to poisoning the dog's system on a monthly basis. Lastly, do not give the pill during the winter months, since there are no mosquitoes around to pass on their infection, unless you live in a tropical environment.

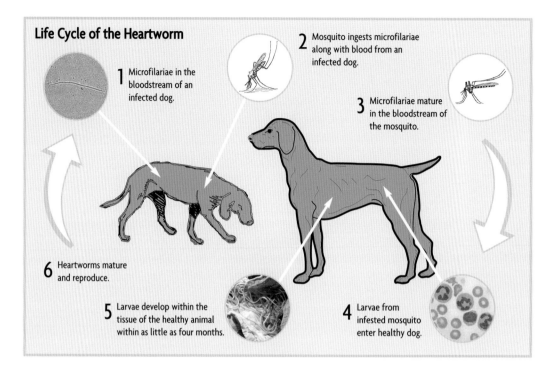

## Life Cycle of the Heartworm

1 Microfilariae in the bloodstream of an infected dog.

2 Mosquito ingests microfilariae along with blood from an infected dog.

3 Microfilariae mature in the bloodstream of the mosquito.

4 Larvae from infested mosquito enter healthy dog.

5 Larvae develop within the tissue of the healthy animal within as little as four months.

6 Heartworms mature and reproduce.

### HEARTWORMS

Heartworms are thin, extended worms up to 12 inches long, which live in a dog's heart and the major blood vessels surrounding it. Dogs may have up to 200 worms. Symptoms may be loss of energy, loss of appetite, coughing, the development of a pot belly and anemia.

Heartworms are transmitted by mosquitoes. The mosquito drinks the blood of an infected dog and takes in larvae with the blood. The larvae, called microfilariae, develop within the body of the mosquito and are passed on to the next dog bitten after the larvae mature. It takes two to three weeks for the larvae to develop to the infective stage within the body of the mosquito. Dogs are usually treated at about six weeks of age and maintained on a prophylactic dose given monthly.

Blood testing for heartworms is not necessarily indicative of how seriously your dog is infected. Although this is a dangerous disease, it is not easy for a dog to be infected. Discuss the various preventatives with your vet, as there are many different types now available. Together you can decide on a safe course of prevention for your dog.

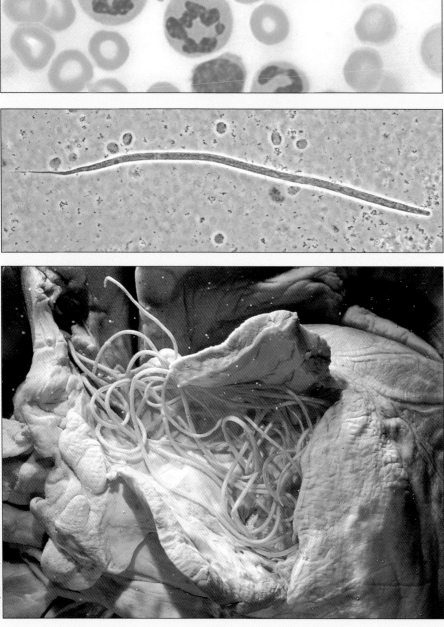

PHOTO BY CAROLINA BIOLOGICAL SUPPLY/PHOTOTAKE.

Magnified heart-worm larvae, *Dirofilaria immitis.*

PHOTO BY JAMES R. HAYDEN, RBP/PHOTOTAKE.

Heartworm, *Dirofilaria immitis.*

PHOTO BY JAMES R. HAYDEN, RBP/PHOTOTAKE.

The heart of a dog infected with canine heart-worm, *Dirofilaria immitis.*

# HOMEOPATHY:
## an alternative to conventional medicine

## "Less is Most"

Using this principle, the strength of a homeopathic remedy is measured by the number of serial dilutions that were undertaken to create it. The greater the number of serial dilutions, the greater the strength of the homeopathic remedy. The potency of a remedy that has been made by making a dilution of 1 part in 100 parts (or 1/100) is 1c or 1cH. If this remedy is subjected to a series of further dilutions, each one being 1/100, a more dilute and stronger remedy is produced. If the remedy is diluted in this way six times, it is called 6c or 6cH. A dilution of 6c is 1 part in 1,000,000,000,000. In general, higher potencies in more frequent doses are better for acute symptoms and lower potencies in more infrequent doses are more useful for chronic, long-standing problems.

## CURING OUR DOGS NATURALLY

Holistic medicine means treating the whole animal as a unique, perfect, living being. Generally, holistic treatments do not suppress the symptoms that the body naturally produces, as do most medications prescribed by conventional doctors and vets. Holistic methods seek to cure disease by regaining balance and harmony in the patient's environment. Some of these methods include use of nutritional therapy, herbs, flower essences, aromatherapy, acupuncture, massage, chiropractic and, of course, the most popular holistic approach, homeopathy.

Homeopathy is a theory or system of treating illness with small doses of substances which, if administered in larger quantities, would produce the symptoms that the patient already has. This approach is often described as "like cures like." Although modern veterinary medicine is geared toward the "quick fix," homeopathy relies on the belief that, given the time, the body is able to heal itself and return to its natural, healthy state.

Choosing a remedy to cure a problem in our dogs is the difficult part of homeopathy. Consult with your vet for a professional diagnosis of your dog's symptoms. Often these symptoms require immediate conventional care. If your vet is willing and knowledgeable, you may attempt a homeopathic remedy. Be aware that cortisone prevents homeopathic remedies from working. There are hundreds of possibilities and combinations to cure many problems in dogs, from basic physical problems such as excessive shedding, fleas or other parasites, unattractive doggy odor, bad breath, upset tummy, obesity, dry, oily or dull coat, diarrhea, ear problems or eye discharge (including tears and dry or mucousy matter), to behavioral abnormalities such as fear of loud noises, habitual licking, poor appetite, excessive barking and various phobias. From alumina to zincum metallicum, the remedies span the planet and the imagination…from flowers and weeds to chemicals, insect droppings, diesel smoke and volcanic ash.

## Using "Like to Treat Like"

Unlike conventional medicines that suppress symptoms, homeopathic remedies treat illnesses with small doses of substances that, if administered in larger quantities, would produce the symptoms that the patient already has. While the same homeopathic remedy can be used to treat different symptoms in different dogs, here are some interesting remedies and their uses.

### Apis Mellifica
(made from honey bee venom) can be used for allergies or to reduce swelling that occurs in acutely infected kidneys.

### Diesel Smoke
can be used to help control travel sickness.

### Calcarea Fluorica
(made from calcium fluoride, which helps harden bone structure) can be useful in treating hard lumps in tissues.

### Natrum Muriaticum
(made from common salt, sodium chloride) is useful in treating thin, thirsty dogs.

### Nitricum Acidum
(made from nitric acid) is used for symptoms you would expect to see from contact with acids, such as lesions, especially where the skin joins the linings of body orifices or openings such as the lips and nostrils.

### Symphytum
(made from the herb Knitbone, *Symphytum officinale*) is used to encourage bones to heal.

### Urtica Urens
(made from the common stinging nettle) is used in treating painful, irritating rashes.

# HOMEOPATHIC REMEDIES FOR YOUR DOG

| Symptom/Ailment | Possible Remedy |
|---|---|
| ALLERGIES | Apis Mellifica 30c, Astacus Fluviatilis 6c, Pulsatilla 30c, Urtica Urens 6c |
| ALOPECIA | Alumina 30c, Lycopodium 30c, Sepia 30c, Thallium 6c |
| ANAL GLANDS (BLOCKED) | Hepar Sulphuris Calcareum 30c, Sanicula 6c, Silicea 6c |
| ARTHRITIS | Rhus Toxicodendron 6c, Bryonia Alba 6c |
| CANINE COUGH | Drosera 6c, Ipecacuanha 30c |
| CATARACT | Calcarea Carbonica 6c, Conium Maculatum 6c, Phosphorus 30c, Silicea 30c |
| CONSTIPATION | Alumina 6c, Carbo Vegetabilis 30c, Graphites 6c, Nitricum Acidum 30c, Silicea 6c |
| COUGHING | Aconitum Napellus 6c, Belladonna 30c, Hyoscyamus Niger 30c, Phosphorus 30c |
| DIARRHEA | Arsenicum Album 30c, Aconitum Napellus 6c, Chamomilla 30c, Mercurius Corrosivus 30c |
| DRY EYE | Zincum Metallicum 30c |
| EAR PROBLEMS | Aconitum Napellus 30c, Belladonna 30c, Hepar Sulphuris 30c, Tellurium 30c, Psorinum 200c |
| EYE PROBLEMS | Borax 6c, Aconitum Napellus 30c, Graphites 6c, Staphysagria 6c, Thuja Occidentalis 30c |
| GLAUCOMA | Aconitum Napellus 30c, Apis Mellifica 6c, Phosphorus 30c |
| HEAT STROKE | Belladonna 30c, Gelsemium Sempervirens 30c, Sulphur 30c |
| HICCOUGHS | Cinchona Deficinalis 6c |
| HIP DYSPLASIA | Colocynthis 6c, Rhus Toxicodendron 6c, Bryonia Alba 6c |
| INCONTINENCE | Argentum Nitricum 6c, Causticum 30c, Conium Maculatum 30c, Pulsatilla 30c, Sepia 30c |
| INSECT BITES | Apis Mellifica 30c, Cantharis 30c, Hypericum Perforatum 6c, Urtica Urens 30c |
| ITCHING | Alumina 30c, Arsenicum Album 30c, Carbo Vegetabilis 30c, Hypericum Perforatum 6c, Mezerium 6c, Sulphur 30c |
| MASTITIS | Apis Mellifica 30c, Belladonna 30c, Urtica Urens 1m |
| MOTION SICKNESS | Cocculus 6c, Petroleum 6c |
| PATELLAR LUXATION | Gelsemium Sempervirens 6c, Rhus Toxicodendron 6c |
| PENIS PROBLEMS | Aconitum Napellus 30c, Hepar Sulphuris Calcareum 30c, Pulsatilla 30c, Thuja Occidentalis 6c |
| PUPPY TEETHING | Calcarea Carbonica 6c, Chamomilla 6c, Phytolacca 6c |

## Recognizing a Sick Dog

Unlike colicky babies and cranky children, our canine kids cannot tell us when they are feeling ill. Therefore, there are a number of signs that owners can identify to know that their dogs are not feeling well.

### Take note for physical manifestations such as:

- unusual, bad odor, including bad breath
- excessive shedding
- wax in the ears, chronic ear irritation
- oily, flaky, dull haircoat
- mucus, tearing or similar discharge in the eyes
- fleas or mites
- mucus in stool, diarrhea
- sensitivity to petting or handling
- licking at paws, scratching face, etc.

### Keep an eye out for behavioral changes as well, including:

- lethargy, idleness
- lack of patience or general irritability
- lack of interest in food
- phobias (fear of people, loud noises, etc.)
- strange behavior, suspicion, fear
- coprophagia
- more frequent barking
- whimpering, crying

## Get Well Soon

You don't need a DVM to provide good TLC to your sick or recovering dog, but you do need to pay attention to some details that normally wouldn't bother him. The following tips will aid Fido's recovery and get him back on his paws again:

- Keep his space free of irritating smells, like heavy perfumes and air fresheners.
- Rest is the best medicine! Avoid harsh lighting that will prevent your dog from sleeping. Shade him from bright sunlight during the day and dim the lights in the evening.
- Keep the noise level down. Animals are more sensitive to sound when they are sick.

- Be attentive to any necessary temperature adjustments. A dog with a fever needs a cool room and cold liquids. A bitch that is whelping or recovering from surgery will be more comfortable in a warm room, consuming warm liquids and food.
- You wouldn't send a sick child back to school early, so don't rush your dog back into a full routine until he seems absolutely ready.

# SILKY TERRIER

The term *old* is a qualitative term. For dogs, as well as their masters, old is relative. Certainly we can all distinguish between a puppy Silky Terrier and an adult Silky Terrier—there are the obvious physical traits, such as size, appearance and coat length, as well as personality traits.

Puppies and young dogs like to play with children. Children's natural exuberance is a good match for the seemingly endless energy of young dogs. They like to run, jump, chase and retrieve. When dogs grow older and cease their interaction with children, they are often thought of as being too old to play with the kids. On the other hand, if a Silky Terrier is only exposed to people who lead quieter lifestyles, his life will normally be less active and the decrease in his activity level as he ages will not be as obvious.

If people live to be 100 years old, dogs live to be 20 years old. While this may sound like a good rule of thumb, it is very inaccurate. When trying to compare dog years to human years, you cannot make a generalization about all dogs. The Silky Terrier is blest with longevity, outliving most other breeds. You can expect that your Silky will live to be 14 to 17 years of age.

Dogs are generally considered mature be three years old, but they can reproduce even earlier. So a more accurate comparison would be that the first three years of a dog's life are like seven times that of a comparable human. That means a 3-year-old dog is like a 21-year-old human. As the curve of comparison shows, however, there is no hard and fast rule for comparing dog and human ages. The comparison is made even more difficult, for not all humans age at the same rate.

## WHAT TO LOOK FOR IN SENIORS

Most vets and behaviorists use the seven-year mark as the time to consider a dog a senior. The term *senior* does not imply that the dog is geriatric and has begun to fail in mind and body. Aging is essentially a slowing process. Humans readily admit that they feel a difference in their activity level from age 20 to 30, and then from 30 to 40, etc. By treating the seven-year-old dog as a senior, owners are able to implement certain therapeutic and preventative medical strategies with the help of their vets. A senior-care program should include at least two veterinary visits per year, screening sessions to determine the dog's health status, as well as nutritional counseling. Vets determine the senior dog's health

For the love and companionship your Silky Terrier provides for his whole life, caring for him in his senior years is a small price to pay.

## AN ANCIENT ACHE

As ancient a disease as any, arthritis remains poorly explained for human and dog alike. Fossils dating back 100 million years show the deterioration caused by arthritis. Human fossils two million years old show the disease in man. The most common type of arthritis affecting dogs is known as osteoarthritis, which occurs in adult dogs before their senior years. Obesity aggravating the dog's joints has been cited as a factor in arthritis.

Rheumatoid disease destroys joint cartilage and causes arthritic joints. Pituitary dysfunctions as well as diabetes have been associated with arthritis. Veterinarians treat arthritis variously, including aspirin, "bed rest" in the dog's crate, physical therapy and exercise, heat therapy (with a heating pad), providing soft bedding materials and treatment with corticosteroids (to reduce pain and swelling temporarily). Your vet will be able to recommend a course of action to help relieve your arthritic pal.

status through a blood smear for a complete blood count, serum chemistry profile with electrolytes, urinalysis, blood pressure check, electrocardiogram, ocular tonometry (pressure on the eyeball) and dental prophylaxis.

Such an extensive program for senior dogs is well advised before owners start to see the obvious physical signs of aging, such as slower and inhibited movement, graying, increased sleep/nap periods and disinterest in play and other activity. This preventative program promises a longer, healthier life for the aging dog. Among the physical problems common in aging dogs are the loss of sight and hearing, arthritis, kidney and liver failure, diabetes mellitus, heart disease and Cushing's disease (a hormonal disease).

In addition to the physical manifestations discussed, there are some behavioral changes and problems related to aging dogs. Dogs suffering from hearing or vision loss, dental discomfort or arthritis can become aggressive. Likewise, the near-deaf and/or blind dog may be startled more easily and react in an unexpectedly aggressive manner. Seniors suffering from senility can become more impatient and irritable. Housesoiling accidents are associated with loss of mobility, kidney problems, loss of sphincter control as well as plaque accumulation, physiological brain changes and reactions to medications. Older dogs, just like young puppies, can suffer from separation anxiety, which can lead to excessive barking, whining, housesoiling and destructive behavior. Seniors may become fearful of everyday sounds, such as vacuum cleaners, heaters, thunder and passing traffic. Some dogs have difficulty sleeping, due to discomfort, the need for frequent toilet visits and the like.

Owners should avoid spoiling the older dog with too many treats. Obesity is a common problem in older dogs and subtracts years from their lives. Keep the senior dog as trim as possible since excess weight puts additional stress on the body's vital organs. Some breeders recommend supplementing the diet with foods high in fiber and lower in calories. Adding fresh vegetables and marrow broth to the senior's diet makes a tasty, low-calorie, low-fat supplement. Vets also offer specialty diets for senior dogs that are worth exploring.

Your dog, as he nears his twilight years, needs his owner's patience and good care more than ever. Never punish an older dog for an accident or abnormal behavior. For all the years of love, protection and companionship that your dog has provided, he deserves special attention and courtesies. The older dog may need to relieve himself at 3 a.m. because he can no longer hold it for eight hours. Older dogs may

Seniors don't keep the same pace they did in their youth. Memories of your swift Silky can become a bit of a blur!

not be able to remain crated for more than two or three hours. It may be time to give up a sofa or chair to your old friend. Although he may not seem as enthusiastic about your attention and petting, he does appreciate the considerations you offer as he gets older.

Your Silky Terrier does not understand why his world is slowing down. Owners must make their dogs' transition into the golden years as pleasant and rewarding as possible.

## WHEN THE TIME COMES

You are never fully prepared to make a rational decision about putting your dog to sleep. It is very obvious that you love your Silky Terrier or you would not be reading this book. Putting a loved dog to sleep is extremely difficult. It is a decision that must be made with your veterinarian. You are usually forced to make the decision when your dog experiences one or more life-threatening symptoms, requiring you to seek veterinary help.

If the prognosis of the malady indicates the end is near and your beloved pet will only suffer more and experience no enjoyment for the balance of his life, then euthanasia is the right choice.

### WHAT *IS* EUTHANASIA?

Euthanasia derives from the Greek, meaning *good death*. In other words, it means the

> **HORMONAL PROBLEMS**
> Although graying is normal and expected in older dogs, a flaky coat or loss of hair is not. Such coat problems may point to a hormonal problem. Hypothyroidism, in which the thyroid gland fails to produce the normal amount of hormones, is one such problem. Your veterinarian can treat hypothyroidism with an oral supplement. The condition is more common in certain breeds, so discuss its likelihood in your dog with your breeder and vet.

planned, painless killing of a dog suffering from a painful, incurable condition, or who is so aged that he cannot walk, see, eat or control his excretory functions.

Euthanasia is usually accomplished by injection with an overdose of an anesthesia or barbiturate. Aside from the prick of the needle, the experience is usually painless.

### MAKING THE DECISION

The decision to euthanize your dog is never easy. The days during which the dog becomes ill and the end occurs can be unusually stressful for you. If this is your first experience with the death of a loved one, you may need the comfort dictated by your religious beliefs. If you are the head of the family and have children, you should have involved them in the

## COPING WITH LOSS

When your dog dies, you may be as upset as when a human companion passes away. You are losing your protector, your baby, your confidante and your best friend. Many people experience not only grief but also feelings of guilt and doubt as to whether they did all that they could for their pet. Allow yourself to grieve and mourn, and seek help from friends and support groups. You may also wish to consult books and websites that deal with this topic.

decision of putting your Silky Terrier to sleep. Usually your dog can be maintained on drugs in the vet's clinic for a few days in order to give you ample time to make a decision. During this time, talking with members of your family or even people who have lived through this same experience can ease the burden of your inevitable decision.

### THE FINAL RESTING PLACE

Dogs can have some of the same privileges as humans. The remains of your beloved dog can be buried in a pet cemetery, which is generally expensive. If your dog has died at home, he can be buried in your yard in a place suitably marked with a stone or a newly planted tree or bush. Alternatively, dogs can be cremated individually and the ashes returned to their

owners. A less expensive option is mass cremation, although, of course, the ashes cannot then be returned. Vets can usually arrange the cremation on your behalf or help you locate a pet cemetery if you choose one of these options. The cost of these options should always be discussed frankly and openly with your vet.

### GETTING ANOTHER DOG?

The grief of losing your beloved dog will be as lasting as the grief of losing a human friend or relative. In most cases, if your dog died of old age (if there is such a thing), he had slowed down considerably. Do you want a new Silky Terrier puppy to replace him? Or are you better off finding a more mature Silky Terrier, say two to three years of age, which will usually be house-trained and will have an already developed personality. In this case, you can find out if you like each other after a few hours of being together.

The decision is, of course, your own. Do you want another Silky Terrier or perhaps a different breed so as to avoid comparison with your beloved friend? Most people usually stay with the same breed because they know and love the characteristics of that breed. Then, too, they often know people who have the same breed and perhaps they are lucky enough that a breeder whom they respect expects a litter soon. What could be better?

# CDS: COGNITIVE DYSFUNCTION SYNDROME
## "Old-Dog Syndrome"

There are many ways for you to evaluate old-dog syndrome. Veterinarians have defined CDS (cognitive dysfunction syndrome) as the gradual deterioration of cognitive abilities. These are indicated by changes in the dog's behavior. When a dog changes his routine response, and maladies have been eliminated as the cause of these behavioral changes, then CDS is the usual diagnosis.

More than half the dogs over eight years old suffer from some form of CDS. The older the dog, the more chance he has of suffering from CDS. In humans, doctors often dismiss the CDS behavioral changes as part of "winding down."

There are four major signs of CDS: frequent potty accidents inside the home, sleeping much more or much less than normal, acting confused and failing to respond to social stimuli.

## SYMPTOMS OF CDS

### FREQUENT POTTY ACCIDENTS
- *Urinates in the house.*
- *Defecates in the house.*
- *Doesn't signal that he wants to go out.*

### SLEEP PATTERNS
- *Awakens more slowly.*
- *Sleeps more than normal during the day.*
- *Sleeps less during the night.*

### CONFUSION
- *Goes outside and just stands there.*
- *Appears confused with a faraway look in his eyes.*
- *Hides more often.*
- *Doesn't recognize friends.*
- *Doesn't come when called.*
- *Walks around listlessly and without a destination.*

### FAILURE TO RESPOND TO SOCIAL STIMULI
- *Comes to people less frequently, whether called or not.*
- *Doesn't tolerate petting for more than a short time.*
- *Doesn't come to the door when you return home.*

As a Silky Terrier owner, you have selected your dog so that you and your loved ones can have a companion, a protector, a friend and a four-legged family member. You invest time, money and effort to care for and train the family's new charge. Of course, this chosen canine behaves perfectly! Well, perfectly like a *dog*.

### THINK LIKE A DOG
Dogs do not think like humans, nor do humans think like dogs, though we try. Unfortunately, a dog is incapable of comprehending how humans think, so the

> ### I'M HOME!
> Dogs left alone for varying lengths of time may often react wildly when their owners return. Sometimes they run, jump, bite, chew, tear things apart, wet themselves, gobble their food or behave in very undisciplined ways. If your dog behaves in this manner upon your return home, allow him to calm down before greeting him or he will consider your attention as a reward for his antics.

responsibility falls on the owner to adopt a viable canine mindset. Dogs cannot rationalize, and dogs exist in the present

Understanding the way canines think is critical to training and modifying behavior. Whether a Silky Terrier or a mixed breed, all dogs behave similarly.

moment. Many a dog owner makes the mistake in training of thinking that he can reprimand his dog for something the dog did a while ago. Basically, you cannot even reprimand a dog for something he did 20 seconds ago! Either catch him in the act or forget it! It is a waste of your and your dog's time—in his mind, you are reprimanding him for whatever he is doing at that moment.

The following behavioral problems represent some which owners most commonly encounter. Every dog is unique and every situation is unique. No author could purport for you to solve your Silky Terrier's problems simply by reading a chapter. Here we outline some basic "dogspeak" so that owners' chances of solving behavioral problems are increased. Discuss bad habits with your vet and he can recommend a behavioral specialist to consult in appropriate cases. Since behavioral abnormalities are the main reason that owners abandon their pets, we hope that you will make a valiant effort to solve your Silky Terrier's problems. Patience and understanding are virtues that must dwell in every pet-loving household.

**SEPARATION ANXIETY**
Your Silky Terrier may howl, whine or otherwise vocalize his

**"LONELY WOLF"**
The number of dogs that suffer from separation anxiety is on the rise as more and more pet owners find themselves at work all day. New attention is being paid to this problem, which is especially hard to diagnose since it is only evident when the dog is alone. Research is currently being done to help educate dog owners about separation anxiety and how they can help minimize this problem in their dogs.

displeasure at your leaving the house and his being left alone. This is a normal reaction, no different than the child who cries as his mother leaves him on the first day at school. Separation anxiety, however, is more serious. In fact, constant attention can lead to separation anxiety in the first place. If you are constantly making a fuss of your dog, he will come to expect this from you all of the time and it will be more traumatic for him when you are not there. Obviously, you enjoy spending time with your dog, and he thrives on your love and attention. However, it should not become a dependent relationship where he is heartbroken without you.

One thing you can do to minimize separation anxiety is to make your entrances and exits as low-key as possible. Do not give your dog a long drawn-out good-bye, and do not lavish him with hugs and kisses when you return. This is giving in to the attention that he craves, and it will only make him miss it more when you are away. Another thing you can try is to give your dog a treat when you leave; this will not only keep him occupied and keep his mind off the fact that you have just left, but it will also help him associate your leaving with a pleasant experience.

You may have to accustom your dog to being left alone in intervals. Of course, when your dog starts whimpering as you

### PHARMACEUTICAL FIX

There are two drugs specifically designed to treat mental problems in dogs. About seven million dogs each year are euthanized because owners can no longer tolerate their dogs' behavior, according to Nicholas Dodman, a specialist in animal behavior at Tufts University in Massachusetts.

The first drug, Clomicalm, is prescribed for dogs suffering from separation anxiety, which is said to cause them to react when left alone by barking, chewing their owners' belongings, drooling copiously or defecating or urinating inside the home.

The second drug, Anipryl, is recommended for cognitive dysfunction syndrome or "old-dog syndrome," a mental deterioration that comes with age. Such dogs often seem to forget that they were housebroken and where their food bowls are, and they may even fail to recognize their owners.

A tremendous human-animal bonding relationship is established with all dogs, particularly senior dogs. This precious relationship deteriorates when the dog does not recognize his master. The drug can restore the bond and make senior dogs feel more like their "old selves."

Silkys generally have a lot to say, and they usually think it's pretty critical that you listen to them. You decide when your Silky's discourse is worthwhile and when it is not.

approach the door, your first instinct will be to run to him and comfort him, but do not do it! Eventually he will adjust to your absence. His anxiety stems from being placed in an unfamiliar situation; by familiarizing him with being alone he will learn that he will survive. That is not to say you should purposely leave your dog home alone, but the dog needs to know that while he can depend on you for his care, you do not have to be by his side 24 hours a day.

When the dog is alone in the house, he should be confined to his crate or designated dog-proof area of the house. This should be the area in which he sleeps and already feels comfortable so he will feel more at ease when he is alone.

*Sniffing and digging go paw in paw. Silkys tend to be curious, adventurous types who don't mind getting their paws dirty for a good time.*

**IT'S PLAY TIME**
Physical games like pulling contests, wrestling, jumping and teasing should not be encouraged. Inciting a dog's crazy behavior tends to confuse him. The owner has to be able to control his dog at all times. Even in play, your dog has to know that you are the leader and that you decide when to play and when to behave mannerly.

**DIGGING**
Digging, which is seen as a destructive behavior to humans, is actually quite a natural behavior in dogs, especially to a dog named after "the earth." Earthdogs, of course, have good reason to want to get their paws dirty! Trying to repress your Silky's desire to dig can be quite a chore for an owner, though careful supervision can solve the problem in no time.

When digging occurs in your yard, it is actually a normal behavior redirected into something the dog can do in his everyday life. In the wild, a dog would be actively seeking food, making his own shelter, etc. He would be using his paws in a purposeful manner for his survival. Since you provide him with food and shelter, he has no need to use his paws for these purposes, and so the energy that he would be using may manifest itself in the form of little holes all over your yard and flower beds. The dog's nose is thousands of times more sensitive than a human's, so it's often difficult to know whether or not your terrier child is smelling rodent droppings or even live mice, rats or the like under the earth. Once a terrier gets a good whiff of a passing rodent, there's not much that can be done to contain his scratching enthusiasm.

Here's where supervision is the best remedy: digging is easiest to control if it is stopped as soon as possible, but it is often hard to catch a dog in the act. If your dog is a compulsive digger and is not easily distracted by other activities, you can designate an area on your property where he is allowed to dig. If you catch him digging in an off-limits area of the yard, immediately bring him to the approved area and praise him for digging there. Keep a close eye on him so that you can catch him in the act—that is the only way to make him understand what is permitted and what is not. If you take him to a hole he dug an hour ago and tell him "No," he will understand that you are not fond of holes, dirt or flowers. If you catch him while he is stifle-deep in your tulips, that is when he will get your message.

## BARKING

Not as yappy as some dogs, and more vocal than others, the Silky Terrier can be a talkative little tyke and, if given the opportunity to express himself, he will certainly make the most of the moment. What exactly is on the Silky's mind is another matter entirely. Indeed, barking is your Silky's way of "talking." It can be somewhat frustrating because it is not always easy to tell what a dog means by his bark—is he excited, happy, frightened or angry? Whatever it is that the dog is trying to say, he should not be punished for barking. It is only when the barking becomes excessive, and when the excessive barking becomes a bad habit, that the behavior needs to be modified.

Fortunately, Silky Terriers, making excellent alarm dogs, tend to use their barks more purposefully, though this is not to say entirely discriminately. If an intruder came into your home in the middle of the night and your

**DOG TALK**
Deciphering your dog's barks is very similar to understanding a baby's cries: there is a different cry for eating, sleeping, potty needs, etc. Your dog talks to you not only through howls and groans but also through his body language. Baring teeth, staring and inflating the chest are all threatening gestures. If a dog greets you by licking his nose, turning his head or yawning, these are friendly, peacemaking gestures.

**BARKING STANCE**
Did you know that a dog is less likely to bark when sitting than standing? Watch your dog the next time that you suspect he is about to start barking. You'll notice that, as he does, he gets up on all four feet. Hence, when teaching a dog to stop barking, it helps to get him to sit before you command him to be quiet.

Silky Terrier barked a warning, wouldn't you be pleased? You would probably deem your dog a hero, a wonderful guardian and protector of the home. On the other hand, if a friend drops by unexpectedly and rings the doorbell and is greeted with a sudden sharp bark, you would probably be annoyed at the dog. But in reality, isn't this just the same behavior? The dog does not know any better...unless he sees who is at the door and it is some-

one he knows, he will bark as a means of vocalizing that his (and your) territory is being threatened. While your friend is not posing a threat, it is all the same to the dog. Barking is his means of letting you know that there is an intrusion, whether friend or foe, on your property. This type of barking is instinctive and should not be discouraged.

Excessive habitual barking, however, is a problem that should be corrected early on. As your Silky Terrier grows up, you will be able to tell when his barking is purposeful and when it is for no reason. You will become able to distinguish your dog's different barks and their meanings. For example, the bark when someone comes to the door will be different than the bark when he is excited to see you. It is similar to a person's tone of voice, except that the dog has to rely totally on tone of voice because he does not have the benefit of using words. An incessant barker will be evident at an early age.

There are some things that encourage a dog to bark. For example, if your dog barks non-stop for a few minutes and you give him a treat to quiet him, he believes that you are rewarding him for barking. He will associate barking with getting a treat, and will keep doing it until he is rewarded.

> **TUG-OF-WAR**
> You should never play tug-of-war games with your puppy. Such games create a struggle for "top dog" position and teach the puppy that it is okay to challenge you. It will also encourage your puppy's natural tendency to bite down hard and *win*.

## AGGRESSION

Silky Terriers are not aggressive, generally speaking, but all dogs that bear the "terrier" appellation in their names have some degree of aggressive tendency flowing within their blue-blooded veins. Aggression, when not controlled, always becomes dangerous. An aggressive dog, no matter the size, may lunge at, bite or even attack a person or another dog. Aggressive behavior is not to be tolerated. It is more than just inappropriate behavior; it is not safe, especially with a tenacious breed such as the Silky Terrier. It is painful for a family to watch their dog become unpredictable in his behavior to the point where they are afraid of him. While not all aggressive behavior is dangerous, things like growling, baring teeth, etc., can be frightening. It is important to ascertain why the dog is acting in this manner. Aggression is a display of dominance, and the dog should not have the dominant role in his pack, which is, in this case, your family.

It is important not to challenge an aggressive dog as this could provoke an attack. Observe your Silky Terrier's body language. Does he make direct eye contact and stare? Does he try to make himself as large as possible: ears pricked, chest out, tail erect? Height and size signify authority in a dog pack—being taller or above another dog literally means that he is above in social status. These body signals tell you that your Silky Terrier thinks he is in charge, a problem

Silkys are most protective of their mistress. Although there may be no warning signs, some dogs can be aggressive when they feel their mistress is being threatened.

that needs to be addressed. An aggressive dog is unpredictable; you never know when he is going to strike and what he is going to do next. You cannot understand why a dog that is playful one minute is growling the next.

If you can isolate what brings out the fear reaction, you can help the dog overcome it. Supervise your Silky Terrier's interactions with people and other dogs, and praise the dog when it goes well. If he starts to act aggressively in a situation, correct him and remove him from the situation. Do not let people approach the dog and start petting him without your express permission. That way, you can have the dog sit to accept petting, and praise him when he behaves properly. You are focusing on praise and on modifying his behavior by rewarding him when he acts appropriately. By being gentle and by supervising his interactions, you are showing him that there is no need to be afraid or defensive.

The best solution is to consult a behavioral specialist, one who has experience with the Silky Terrier if possible. Together, perhaps you can pinpoint the cause of your dog's aggression and do something about it. An aggressive dog cannot be trusted, and a dog that cannot be trusted is not safe to have as a family pet. If, very unusually, you find that your pet has become untrustworthy and you feel it necessary to seek a new home with a more suitable family and environment, explain fully to the new owners all of your reasons for rehoming the dog to be fair to all concerned. In the *very worst* case, you will have to consider euthanasia.

**AGGRESSION TOWARD OTHER DOGS**
A dog's aggressive behavior toward another dog sometimes stems from insufficient exposure to other dogs at an early age. If

---

### BELLY UP!

When two dogs are introduced, they will naturally establish who is dominant. This may involve one dog placing his front paws on the other's shoulders, or one dog rolling over and exposing his belly, thereby assuming a submissive status. If neither dog submits, they may fight until one has been pinned down. This behavior can be upsetting for owners to watch, especially if your dog takes one look and throws himself on the ground. The biggest mistake you can make is to interfere, pulling on the leads and confusing the dogs. If you don't allow them to establish their pecking order, you undermine the pack mentality, which can cause your dog great stress. If you separate dogs in the middle of a fight, the interference may incite them to attack each other viciously. Your best choice is to stay out of it!

other dogs make your Silky nervous and agitated, he will lash out as a defensive mechanism, though this behavior is thankfully uncommon in the breed. A dog who has not received sufficient exposure to other canines tends to believe that he is the only dog on the continent. The animal becomes so dominant that he does not even show signs that he is fearful or threatened. Without growling or any other physical signal as a warning, he will lunge at and bite the other dog.

A way to correct this is to let your Silky Terrier approach another dog when walking on lead. Watch very closely and at the very first sign of aggression, correct your Silky Terrier and pull him away. Scold him for any sign of discomfort, and then praise him when he ignores or tolerates the other dog. Keep this up until he stops the aggressive behavior, learns to ignore the other dog or accepts other dogs. Praise him lavishly for his correct behavior.

### DOMINANT AGGRESSION

A social hierarchy is firmly established in a wild dog pack. The dog wants to dominate those under him and please those above him. Dogs know that there must be a leader. If you are not the obvious choice for emperor, the dog will assume the throne!

---

**SOUND BITES**

When a dog bites, there is always a good reason for his doing so. Many dogs are trained to protect a person, an area or an object. When that person, area or object is violated, the dog will attack. A dog attacks with his mouth. He has no other means of attack.

Fighting dogs (and there are many breeds that fight, though the Silky is not one such breed) are taught to fight, but they also have a natural instinct to fight. This instinct is normally reserved for other dogs, though unfortunate accidents can occur; for example, when a baby crawls toward a fighting dog and the dog mistakes the crawling child as a potential attacker.

If a dog is a biter for seemingly no reason, if he bites the hand that feeds him or if he snaps at members of your family, see your veterinarian or behaviorist immediately to learn how to modify the dog's behavior.

---

These conflicting innate desires are what a dog owner confronts when he sets about training a dog. In training a dog to obey commands, the owner is reinforcing that he is the top dog in the pack and that the dog should, and should want to, serve his superior. Thus, the owner is suppressing the dog's urge to dominate by modifying his behavior and making him obedient.

## "X" MARKS THE SPOT

As a pack animal, your dog marks his territory as a way of letting any possible intruders know that this is his space and that he will defend his territory if necessary. Your dog marks by urinating because urine contains pheromones that allow other canines to identify him. While this behavior seems like a nuisance, it speaks volumes about your dog's mental health. Stable, well-trained dogs living in quiet, less populated areas may mark less frequently than less confident dogs inhabiting busy urban areas that attract many possible invaders. If your dog only marks in certain areas in your home, your bed or just the front door, these are the areas he feels obligated to defend. If your dog marks frequently, see your veterinarian or an animal behaviorist.

An important part of training is taking every opportunity to reinforce that you are the leader. The simple action of making your Silky Terrier sit to wait for his food says that you control when he eats and that he is dependent on you for food. Although it may be difficult, do not give in to your dog's wishes every time he whines at you or looks at you with his pleading eyes. It is a constant effort to show the dog that his place in the pack is at the bottom. This is not meant to sound cruel or inhumane. You love your Silky Terrier and you should treat him with care and affection. You (hopefully) did not get a dog just so you could control another creature. Dog training is not about being cruel, it is about molding the dog's behavior into what is acceptable and teaching him to live by your rules. In theory, it is quite simple: catch him in appropriate behavior and reward him for it. Add a dog into the equation and it becomes a bit more trying, but as a rule of thumb, positive reinforcement is what works best.

With a dominant dog, punishment and negative reinforcement can have the opposite effect from what you desire. It can make a dog fearful and/or act out aggressively if he feels he is being challenged. Remember, a dominant dog perceives himself

## THE MIGHTY MALE

Males, whether castrated or not, will mount almost anything: a pillow, your leg or, much to your dismay, even your neighbor's leg. As with other types of inappropriate behavior, the dog must be corrected while in the act, which for once is not difficult. Often he will not let go! While a puppy is experimenting with his very first urges, his owners feel he needs to "sow his oats" and allow the pup to mount. As the pup grows into a full-size dog, with full-size urges, it becomes a nuisance and an embarrassment. Males always appear as if they are trying to "save the race," more determined and stronger than imaginable. While altering the dog at an appropriate age will limit the dog's desire, it usually does not remove it entirely.

methods; scolding is necessary now and then, but the focus in your training should always be on positive reinforcement.

### SEXUAL BEHAVIOR

Dogs exhibit certain sexual behaviors that may have influenced your choice of male or female when you first purchased your Silky Terrier. To a certain extent, spaying/neutering will eliminate these behaviors, but if you are purchasing a dog that you wish to breed from, you should be aware of what you will have to deal with throughout the dog's life.

Female dogs usually have two estruses per year with each season lasting about three weeks. These are the only times in which a female dog will mate, and she usually will not allow

at the top of the social heap and will fight to defend his perceived status. The best way to prevent that is never to give him reason to think that he is in control in the first place. If you are having trouble training your Silky Terrier and it seems as if he is constantly challenging your authority, seek the help of an obedience trainer or behavioral specialist. A professional will work with both you and your dog to teach you effective techniques to use at home. Beware of trainers who rely on excessively harsh

Your selection of a male or female Silky may be based on certain sexual characteristics. Both sexes tend to be protective of their owners, though males may be more vigilant in their watchkeeping.

this until the second week of the cycle, but this does vary from bitch to bitch. If not bred during the heat cycle, it is not uncommon for a bitch to experience a false pregnancy, in which her mammary glands swell and she exhibits maternal tendencies toward toys or other objects.

Owners must further recognize that mounting is not merely a sexual expression but also one of dominance seen in males and females alike. Be consistent and persistent and you will find that you can "move mounters."

### CHEWING

The national canine pastime is chewing! Every dog loves to sink his "canines" into a tasty bone,

and the owner must provide his dog with appropriate chew devices. Dogs need to chew, to massage their gums, to make their new teeth feel better and to exercise their jaws. This is a natural behavior deeply embedded in all things canine. Our role as owners is not to stop the dog's

Often a dog's chewing needs can be satisfied with a safe chew toy, but more frequently the Silky will select your shoe or slipper because it bears your scent. Keep your possessions out of the reach of the Silky's teeth.

chewing, but to redirect it to positive, chew-worthy objects. Be an informed owner and purchase proper chew toys like strong nylon bones that will not splinter. Be sure that the objects are safe and durable, since your dog's safety is at risk. Again, the owner is responsible for ensuring a dog-proof environment.

The best answer is prevention, that is, put your shoes, handbags and other tasty objects in their proper places (out of the reach of the growing canine mouth). Direct your puppy to his toys whenever you see him tasting the furniture legs or the leg of your pants. Make a loud noise to attract the pup's attention and immediately escort him to his chew toy and engage him with the toy for at least four minutes, praising and encouraging him all the while.

Some trainers recommend deterrents, such as hot pepper, a bitter spice or a product

## NO JUMPING

Stop a dog from jumping up before he jumps. If he is getting ready to jump onto you, simply walk away. If he jumps up on you before you can turn away, lift your knee so that it bumps him in the chest. Do not be forceful. Your dog soon will realize that jumping up is not a productive way of getting attention.

designed for this purpose, to discourage the dog from chewing unwanted objects. Test these products yourself before investing in large quantities.

### JUMPING UP

Jumping up is a dog's friendly way of saying hello! Some dog owners do not mind when their

Terriers have strong hind legs and can jump very high. No matter how amusing a game of leapfrog may seem, don't encourage your Silky to develop bad habits.

Canine beggars are a nuisance, no matter how charming and desperate they appear. Don't feed your dog from the table or you will teach him to beg.

dog jumps up. The problem arises when guests come to the house and the dog greets them in the same manner—whether they like it or not! However friendly the greeting may be, the chances are that your visitors will not appreciate your dog's enthusiasm. The dog will not be able to distinguish upon whom he can jump and whom he cannot. Therefore, it is probably best to discourage this behavior entirely.

Pick a command such as "Off" (avoid using "Down" since you will use that for the dog to lie down) and tell him "Off" when he jumps up. Place him on the ground on all fours and have him sit, praising him the whole time. Always lavish him with praise and petting when he is in the sit position. In this way you can give him a warm affectionate greeting, let him know that you are as pleased to see him as he is to see you and instill good manners at the same time!

## NO KISSES

We all love our dogs and our dogs love us. They show their love and affection by licking us. This is not a very sanitary practice, as dogs lick and sniff in some unsavory places. Kissing your dog on the mouth is strictly forbidden, as parasites can be transmitted in this manner.

## FOOD STEALING

Is your dog devising ways of stealing food from your coffee table? If so, you must answer the following questions: Is your Silky Terrier hungry, or is he "constantly famished" like many dogs seem to be? Face it, some dogs are more food-motivated than others. They are totally obsessed by the smell of food and can only think of their next meal. Food stealing is terrific fun and always yields a great reward—*food*, glorious food.

The owner's goal, therefore, is to be sensible about where food is placed in the home, and to reprimand your dog whenever he is caught in the act of stealing. But remember, only reprimand your dog if you actually see him stealing, not later when

The victory lap! Your Silky should never get this close to your dinner plate, or else you will be the loser every time.

the crime is discovered, for that will be of no use at all and will only serve to confuse him.

**BEGGING**
Just like food stealing, begging is a favorite pastime of hungry puppies! It achieves that same terrific result—*food!* Dogs quickly learn that their owners keep the "good food" for

ourselves, and that we humans do not dine on dry food alone. Begging is a conditioned response related to a specific stimulus, time and place. The sounds of the kitchen, cans and bottles opening, crinkling bags, the smell of food in preparation, etc., will excite the dog, and soon the paws are in the air!

Here is the solution to stop-

**THE ORIGIN OF THE DINNER BELL**
The study of animal behavior can be traced back to the 1800s and the renowned psychologist, Pavlov. When it was time for his dogs to eat, Pavlov would ring a bell, then feed the dogs. Pavlov soon discovered that the dogs learned to associate the bell with food and would drool at the sound of a bell. And you thought yours was the only dog obsessed with eating!

ping this behavior: Never give in to a beggar! You are rewarding the dog for sitting pretty, jumping up, whining and rubbing his nose into you by giving him food. By ignoring the dog, you will (eventually) force the behavior into extinction. Note that the behavior is likely to get worse before it disappears, so be sure there are not any "softies" in the family who will give in to little "Oliver" every time he whimpers, "More, please."

## COPROPHAGIA

Feces eating is, to humans, one of the most disgusting behaviors that their dog could engage in, yet to the dog it is perfectly normal. It is hard for us to understand why a dog would want to eat his own feces. He could be seeking certain nutrients that are missing from his diet, he could be just plain hungry or he could be attracted by the pleasing (to a dog) scent. While coprophagia most often refers to the dog eating his own feces, a dog may just as likely eat that of another animal as well if he comes across it. Dogs often find the stool of cats and horses more palatable than that of other dogs.

Vets have found that diets with a low digestibility, containing relatively low levels of fiber and high levels of starch, increase coprophagia. Therefore,

high-fiber diets may decrease the likelihood of dogs' eating feces. Both the consistency of the stool (how firm it feels in the dog's mouth) and the presence of undigested nutrients increase the likelihood. Once the dog develops diarrhea from feces eating, he will likely stop this distasteful habit.

A talented chow hound doing the dance of the seven victuals!

---

**DOGS HAVE FEELINGS, TOO**

You probably don't realize how much your dog notices the presence of a new person in your home as well as the loss of a familiar face. If someone new has moved in with you, your pet will need help adjusting. Have the person feed your dog or accompany the two of you on a walk. Also, make sure your roommate is aware of the rules and routines you have already set for your dog.

If you have just lost a longtime companion, there is a chance you could end up with a case of "leave me, leave my dog." Dogs experience separation anxiety and depression, so watch for any changes in sleeping and eating habits and try to lavish a little extra love on your dog. It might make you feel better, too.

---

To discourage this behavior, first make sure that the food you are feeding your dog is nutritionally complete and that he is getting enough food. If changes in his diet do not seem to work, and no medical cause can be found, you will have to modify the behavior through environmental control before it becomes a habit. The best way to prevent your dog from eating his stool is to make it unavailable—clean up after he eliminates and remove any stool

Keen, alert and intelligent, the nature of the Silky Terrier shows in the breed's inquisitive expression and sparkling eyes.

With proper care, responsible training and a lot of love, your Silky Terrier will grow up to be an affectionate, obedient companion. You have many years of rewards to look forward to.

from your backyard. If it is not there, he cannot eat it.

Reprimanding for stool eating rarely impresses the dog. Vets recommend distracting the dog while he is in the act of stool eating. Coprophagia is seen most frequently in pups 6 to 12 months of age, and usually disappears around the dog's first birthday.

## BE NOT AFRAID

Just like humans, dogs can suffer from phobias, including fear of thunder, fear of heights, fear of stairs or even fear of specific objects such as the swimming pool. To help your dog get over his fear, first determine what is causing the phobia. For example, your dog may be generalizing by associating an accident that occurred on one set of stairs with every step he sees. You can try desensitization training, which involves introducing the fear-trigger to your dog slowly, in a relaxed setting, and rewarding him when he remains calm. Most importantly, when your dog responds fearfully, do not coddle or try to soothe him, as this only makes him think that his fear is okay.

# INDEX

# My Silky Terrier

PUT YOUR PUPPY'S FIRST PICTURE HERE

Dog's Name _____

Date _____ Photographer _____